P9-EEP-000

Loyal No More

JOHN IBBITSON

Loyal No More

Ontario's Struggle for a Separate Destiny

A Phyllis Bruce Book
HarperCollins*PublishersLtd*

Loyal No More:
Ontario's Struggle for a Separate Destiny

For information address HarperCollins Publishers Ltd,
55 Avenue Road, Suite 2900,
Toronto, Ontario, Canada M5R 3L2

www.harpercanada.com

HarperCollins books may be purchased for educational, business, or sales promotional use. For information please write: Special Markets Department,
HarperCollins Canada,
55 Avenue Road, Suite 2900,
Toronto, Ontario, Canada M5R 3L2

First edition

The author wishes to thank the following for permission to reproduce photographs:
The Canadian Heritage Gallery:
George Brown (ID #20707); John A. Macdonald (ID #21943); the Interprovincial Conference at Quebec City, 1887 (ID #20149); Edward Blake (ID #20738); Trudeaumania (ID #21035)
The Canadian Press Archives:
Sir Oliver Mowat (ID #914679); The Dominion-Provincial Conference of 1927 (ID #880193); Sir Robert Borden (ID #861097); W.L.M. King and Mitchell Hepburn (ID #909103); Leslie Frost and Allen Lamport (ID #925430); John Robarts (ID #1201408); Pierre Trudeau and Bill Davis (ID #1804551); Mike Harris, Bob Rae and David Peterson (ID #1009923); Mike Harris, Ralph Klein and Lucien Bouchard (ID #155582); Stockwell Day (ID #1948644)
The Ontario Archives:
George Drew and members of Cabinet (Acc. #2513 s. 85)

Canadian Cataloguing in Publication Data

Ibbitson, John
Loyal no more :
Ontario's struggle for a separate destiny

"A Phyllis Bruce book".
ISBN 0-00-200030-X

1. Ontario – Politics and government.
2. Federal-provincial relations – Ontario.*
3. Ontario – History.
I. Title.

FC3061.122 2001 971.3 C00-932352-X
F1058.122 2001

01 02 03 04 HC 4 3 2 1

Printed and bound in the United States
Set in Monotype Perpetua

JOHN IBBITSON

Loyal No More

Ontario's Struggle for a Separate Destiny

A Phyllis Bruce Book
HarperCollins*PublishersLtd*

For information address HarperCollins Publishers Ltd,
55 Avenue Road, Suite 2900,
Toronto, Ontario, Canada M5R 3L2

www.harpercanada.com

HarperCollins books may be purchased for educational, business, or sales promotional use. For information please write: Special Markets Department,
HarperCollins Canada,
55 Avenue Road, Suite 2900,
Toronto, Ontario, Canada M5R 3L2

First edition

The author wishes to thank the following for permission to reproduce photographs:
The Canadian Heritage Gallery:
George Brown (ID #20707); John A. Macdonald (ID #21943); the Interprovincial Conference at Quebec City, 1887 (ID #20149); Edward Blake (ID #20738); Trudeaumania (ID #21035)
The Canadian Press Archives:
Sir Oliver Mowat (ID #914679); The Dominion-Provincial Conference of 1927 (ID #880193); Sir Robert Borden (ID #861097); W.L.M. King and Mitchell Hepburn (ID #909103); Leslie Frost and Allen Lamport (ID #925430); John Robarts (ID #1201408); Pierre Trudeau and Bill Davis (ID #1804551); Mike Harris, Bob Rae and David Peterson (ID #1009923); Mike Harris, Ralph Klein and Lucien Bouchard (ID #15582); Stockwell Day (ID #1948644)
The Ontario Archives:
George Drew and members of Cabinet (Acc. #2513 s. 85)

Canadian Cataloguing in Publication Data

Ibbitson, John
Loyal no more :
Ontario's struggle for a separate destiny

"A Phyllis Bruce book".
ISBN 0-00-200030-X

1. Ontario – Politics and government.
2. Federal-provincial relations – Ontario.*
3. Ontario – History.
I. Title.

FC3061.I22 2001 971.3 C00-932352-X
F1058.I22 2001

01 02 03 04 HC 4 3 2 1

Printed and bound in the United States
Set in Monotype Perpetua

In memory of the settler families—
the Heidmans and Boyds in particular—
who first broke the stone-laced soil
of the Muskoka District

Contents

Loyal No More

INTRODUCTION

Accounting for Ontario

Nothing so warms the heart of a politician as a plant expansion, especially the expansion of an auto plant, cornerstone of the Ontario economy. Both men were there to bask in the rising sun of Ontario's latest coup: the addition of a third shift to the Chrysler assembly line in Brampton. And both men had every reason to congratulate themselves and each other. In 1993 Jean Chrétien had inherited a federal government headed for bankruptcy, with debt and deficits so high that, as incoming prime minister, he feared the International Monetary Fund might need to intervene. Four years later the deficit was vanishing, growth was strong, unemployment was falling, and his Liberal government enjoyed a popularity, even affection, among Canadians reminiscent of the days of Louis St. Laurent. In 1995 Mike Harris had inherited an Ontario government that was spending a million dollars an hour more than it was taking in, where the unemployment rate in St. Catharines had at one point surpassed that of St. John's, where chronic political mismanagement was threatening to undermine the very foundations of one of the most prosperous places in North America. Two years later, not only had he brought the deficit under control but the Conservatives' broad-based program of tax cuts and industrial deregulation had helped reverse the province's stagnant fortunes and restored Ontario's economic primacy and sense of confidence. It was, in other words, a good time for both men to pat each other on the back.

Instead, they sat through the speeches stone-faced, each barely acknowledging the other's presence. Their handshake was brief, perfunctory, as though painful to the touch. They separated at the first possible moment, heading to their respective corners, where the reporters were waiting.

Ottawa and Toronto were at war. The federal, provincial, and territorial governments had recently agreed to offer limited compensation to those who had contracted hepatitis C through the Canadian blood supply after 1985. But the deal outraged the public, as well as the victims, by excluding those infected before 1986 for what were, in essence, legalistic reasons. For a few weeks the federal and provincial governments had jointly defended the deal, but now Ontario had joined Ottawa's ancient adversary, Quebec, in demanding that the package be reopened. The Harris government's betrayal of the original agreement was only the latest, and most galling, in a string of confrontations between Queen's Park and Parliament Hill that had left Ontario-federal relations more embittered than at any time since the Second World War.

Chrétien was clearly irritated by Harris's attitude and by the uncomfortable questions coming at him from journalists. Why wouldn't the federal government extend the compensation for hep C victims? Why wouldn't it reopen negotiations with the provinces? Why was he being so unfair? The prime minister lashed back: ask Mike Harris why the Ontario government was not offering more money, while expecting the federal government to expand compensation. "He has no money for the people who are suffering in Ontario," Chrétien fumed, "but he has $5 billion for tax cuts, mostly for the people who are doing quite well."[1] When Harris learned of the prime minister's remarks, his face reddened. The Ontario government was battling to sustain its health care system, despite billions of dollars in slashed transfers from Ottawa.

And now Chrétien dared to link tax cuts to compensation for the hep C victims? When the premier's airplane landed in Owen Sound, local reporters were treated to a big-city scoop. "I have asked our legal people to take a look at whether there is cause for the Ontario government to take action against the Red Cross and against the federal government,"[2] Harris told a Chamber of Commerce dinner. Ontario was ready to sue, but the premier had decided to go much farther: he would renege on the federal-provincial deal and unilaterally offer $200 million in compensation to Ontario hep C victims infected before 1986. Ottawa's position became infinitely more embarrassing when the Ontario government declared its resolve several days later. Chrétien and his health minister, Allan Rock, would suffer through weeks of bad press, opposition assaults, and public anger, thanks to Harris's decision to bail out of the joint agreement.

This dispute between the Ontario and the federal governments was more than an isolated incident. It was more than part of a steadily deteriorating relationship between two politicians competing for the affection of Ontario voters. Rather, it was a signpost along a long road, a road that may end in a fork, with Ontario going one way and the rest of Canada, another. Ontario is becoming estranged from Confederation. The most visible manifestation of that estrangement is the growing rift between Queen's Park and Parliament Hill.

Such sentiments may seem strange, for Ontario has no history of separatism. True, some of Toronto's hotter-headed municipal politicians have talked about the city seceding, and northern Ontarians have wondered at times whether southern Ontario knew or cared about their special concerns. But no one has ever stood up and declared, "I am an Ontario separatist."

To be a separatist, one must have a sense of self and a sense of grievance. Quebecers, who possess an excess of both, have been contemplating their departure from the federation for decades, and on two occasions have almost made up their minds to quit the nation. Westerners, who feel themselves in thrall to the big-money interests of central Canada, look south and west far more comfortably than east. Atlantic Canadians have grieved over the loss of their status and wealth for a century and a half. Only Ontarians (the very word sits uncomfortably on the tongue) appear to be unaware of themselves and content with the status quo. Traditionally, Ontarians have identified themselves as Canadians more readily than citizens from any other part of Canada, with the possible exception of New Brunswickers.

This acceptance of Ontario's complacency, however, ignores history. Through much of its existence, the province has been a principal antagonist of the federal government. In one sense, Ontario is engaged in a struggle to return to its former self.

The first European settlers who ventured into the region, discovering the fabulous richness of its soils, displacing the well-entrenched Native societies, and establishing the farms, villages, towns, and cities of southern Ontario, believed in God, hard work, and the Reform Party—the protector of Protestantism, property, and the principle of one man, one vote. The land rewarded their righteousness, first in a bonanza of wheat, then in a great industrial state. Ontario has always been the richest and most optimistic of the provinces, the quintessential pioneer province, the first and only imperial province, with territorial and economic ambitions to the north and west, the province with the population and the wealth to get its own way. The legacy of the nineteenth-century farmers from Elgin County is taken up today by arrivals from Taiwan, as they set out to mine the province's still-untapped wealth. Certain writers have mistakenly characterized the root metaphor of Ontario culture as one of survival, of isolation within a hostile and unforgiving nature. Not so: the root metaphor of Ontario is success.

The good fortune that attended the efforts of the province's first settlers bequeathed a feeling not only of optimism but of centredness.

This characteristic bound the colony together in its early years, and it binds the province together to this day. At its worst this centredness manifests itself in condescending arrogance towards others; at its best it pushes the province's 11 million people to build on their predecessors' success. It defines Ontarians as they are.

In politics, this sense of centredness has revealed itself in an impatient insistence on freedom. Upper Canadians and Ontarians were, and are, among the freest people on earth. Even in the first half of the nineteenth century the franchise was widely held. All male landowners could vote, and most adult males owned land. In England the property qualification disenfranchised most of the population, while in the United States every man could vote who wasn't a slave. (Women, of course, did not yet have the franchise.) Upper Canadians are used to being free, to having their say, to having what they say listened to by the powers that be.

From the time of Confederation until the 1940s, successive Ontario governments struggled to limit the power of the federal government to encroach on the province's freedom of action. Ontario, as well as Quebec, demanded the right to be left alone. After the Second World War, however, Queen's Park and Ottawa collaborated to ensure that the rest of the federation served the interests of the economic heartland. That symbiosis dissolved in the 1980s and 1990s, dissipated by federal deficits, provincial intransigence, and Ottawa's blinkered obsession with Quebec. And other even more important forces were at work: free trade, which both invigorated and reoriented Ontario's economy, the increasing irrelevance of interprovincial commerce, and the internal contradictions of the national taxation system.

Today, a federal government that depends for its existence on extracting the wealth of Ontario—and to a lesser extent of Alberta and British Columbia—and redistributing it to poorer parts of Canada finds itself in perpetual conflict with an Ontario government determined to assert its people's interests, protect their taxes, and rule within its own house. A federation so constructed cannot endure.

The challenge to Confederation lies not simply in accommodating Quebec's ancient and frustrated nationhood, the Maritimes' sense of enforced dependence, or the West's geographical and political alienation. The biggest and most powerful region of all now demands: first you must account for me.

Accounting for Ontario will become the greatest and most intractable challenge to Confederation, one that will change the federation, incrementally but inexorably, over the coming years. No one should say with confidence that the federation as we know it will survive. Everyone should presume that, whatever the outcome, Ontario will have its way.

Toronto
December 2000

I

"Some Joint Authority"

Day had turned to dark and still they argued. The steady glow of the gas lamps along the wall and the cut-glass splendour of the chandelier overhead illuminated a fog of cigar smoke and oratory. Toronto's proud new St. Lawrence Town Hall could barely hold their numbers, more than five hundred in all, pressed together, collars wilted, their bodies warming the room against the November cold. Some listened quietly to the impassioned pleas from speakers who mounted the platform one after another, several shouted questions and objections, others argued heatedly among themselves, while many simply jeered and cheered for mischief. The Reform Convention of 1859, called to determine the future of Upper Canada, was disintegrating: those who favoured dissolution were gaining ground, and those who argued for a federation of provinces were worried and uncertain. The question now was whether George Brown could reseal the rift.

It was Brown's convention, after all. He had called it, organized it, manipulated its committees, shaped its resolutions. But he could not guarantee its outcome. Upper Canadian Reformers had always been a fractious and independent-minded bunch, which was what made them Reformers. There were the southwestern Clear Grits, fervent exponents of so pure a democracy that the governor general himself would be an elected official if they had their way. Some even favoured union with the United States, which they saw as the ultimate democracy, even if the Republic did appear to be sliding into civil war over slavery and states' rights. Others were simple dissolutionists, sick of the forced union of English, Protestant Upper Canada with French, Catholic Lower Canada, which they were convinced was a nest of papist conspiracies. There were moderates, too: well-padded Toronto businessmen and south-central farmers who abhorred the corruption and paralysis of the union government, but who feared dissolution because it might deliver exclusive control of the St. Lawrence River to Quebec, blocking Upper Canadian access to overseas markets. There were even a few from the conservative eastern counties who weren't certain that the union had to be dissolved at all: could it not simply be improved?

All of them, whatever their views, acknowledged George Brown as their leader. Ever since he had founded the *Globe* fifteen years earlier, in 1844, the newspaper proprietor and politician had been the principled, passionate voice of reform in Upper Canada. In closely argued editorials, in lengthy, passionate speeches in the Assembly, on the hustings during elections, and in countless political meetings across the province, Brown had voiced the discontents of the prosperous colony, the virtues of representation by population, the need to loosen the forced union with Quebec and with Great Britain. God knows he was stiff-necked, his self-righteous Scottish intransigence better suited to expounding principles than making political deals. His unwillingness to compromise had kept him out of the premier's chair, even though Reformers of one shape or another had dominated the Canada West half of the Assembly for years. In his one brief moment of glory, in 1858, when he had forged a deal with the Quebec liberals (the *rouges*) to unseat the wily partnership of John A. Macdonald and George-Étienne Cartier, his administration had lasted for only two days before he was outmanoeuvred by the hated duo.

Even though the defeat had left his supporters despondent, there was no one for them but Brown—no one who had the power of a *Globe* to champion their cause, whose rigidity of purpose could satisfy the Clear Grits, but whose intelligence and loyalty to the crown could reassure the moderates. If Brown couldn't hold them together and lead them to power, no one could. But could he? And if they ever did win power, what would they do with it?

The Reformers knew they must make choices. Did they still want Brown as their leader? Was there no way to end the corrupt coalition between the minority Upper Canadian conservatives and the majority French conservatives (the *bleus*) that dominated the Province of Canada? And if it could be ended, what should replace it? Was there any kind of federation with Canada East (Lower Canada) that would benefit Canada West (Upper Canada)? Or was it time to go it alone, to seek a separate destiny within North America? These fundamental questions needed to be answered. Brown had answers to them, but before he could carry those answers forward, he required the endorsement of all the partners in the Reform coalition. They could not be forced, they could not be coerced. They could only be coaxed, and he would have to coax them.

But his plan wasn't working. The colony's brief but tumultuous history was getting in the way.

The glaciers that scraped their way across the upper half of North America carved out a basin of lakes that framed Ontario's borders and served as a vital transportation corridor, while also depositing within the broad southern peninsula separating those lakes some of the richest soil in North America. The 50,000 Indians of the Algonkian and Iroquoian languages who inhabited what is now Ontario made little dent in its canopied forests, and French explorers and fur traders venturing into the region in the seventeenth and early eighteenth centuries were more interested in furs than farming. The province's modern history emerged from the detritus of the American Revolution: thousands of Americans who had remained loyal to the British throne were voluntarily or forcibly dispossessed by the republican victory of 1783; and thousands of British soldiers, having lost the war, found themselves with nothing to do and no great desire to return to an overcrowded Great Britain.

About six thousand of them meandered into the unsettled British lands of what was called Upper Canada—since it was upriver from Lower Canada, or Quebec—settling along the north shore of the St. Lawrence River, on the eastern end of Lake Ontario, and in the Niagara Peninsula. These first Loyalist settlers quickly discovered they had hit pay dirt. Southwestern and south-central Ontario, together with parts in the southeast, offer perfect growing conditions for wheat, which was badly needed in nineteenth-century Great Britain. The Atlantic colonies had poor soil and a wet climate. The soil of Lower Canada and the northeastern United States had been exhausted through overcultivation. The great mid-west of the continent remained largely a mystery. But here, in the new lands between the Great Lakes, was soil so fertile that the first settlers were able to bring in crops even before they had cleared their fields, simply by planting around the trees. Ontario would be built on wheat.

In an astonishingly few years a torrent of settlers invaded the new territory—the broad flat plain framed by the St. Lawrence and Ottawa rivers; the smaller lake area north from Lake Ontario; the rich, warm Niagara Peninsula and the rolling farmland north of Lake Erie; and, finally, the more northern soils east of Lake Huron and south of Georgian Bay. They forced primitive roads through the forest, staked out their land, felled or burned the trees, threw up crude log cabins, and brought in their first crops. Then they began to improve—to lay out stone and split-rail fences, uproot the stumps that marred their fields, add more land to their original claim, and build more substantial homes. A single settler could clear between five and ten acres a year.

In the space of a lifetime, the colony was transformed from virgin forest into a prosperous, thriving settlement. The population swelled from a few scattered settlers in 1783 to 77,000 men, women, and children at the outbreak of the War of 1812, when the United States tried, but failed, to add the British colonies to its own burgeoning empire. By 1850 the southern portion of the province was fully settled and the land cleared, with the population standing at 950,000. The province was thriving. Wars, British tariffs, periodic droughts, and financial depressions notwithstanding, Upper Canada was a wheat-producing machine of amazing efficiency. By 1800 the colony was exporting around 75,000 bushels of wheat in a good year, and by 1845, in excess of 2 million bushels. In 1861 the total peaked at more than 12 million bushels a year.

The population spread evenly, the towns growing in proportion to the farms that sustained them. Elsewhere in British North America a single great city dominated a largely rural countryside: Montreal in Quebec, Halifax in Nova Scotia. But in Upper Canada, although York was unquestionably the first city in terms of finance, politics, and society, the new colony boasted a true matrix of settlement.

This matrix was by no means uniform. Late-arriving Irish and German immigrants struggled with marginal land, rocky soil, and rotting stumps. They lived on salt pork in tiny, smoky, drafty log cabins and were tortured by isolation and blackflies. But within a few miles of such misery, a township of settled farms on fine land, complete with wood-frame or brick houses, might line a newly improved road, as families travelled in horse-drawn carts to the nearest town for supplies on Saturday and church on Sunday. The men and women who farmed these lands were generally of Loyalist or British immigrant stock, fiercely Protestant in religion, and imbued with the virtues of hard work. The province was too new, and the population too thin, to sustain a landed gentry. No one, no matter how affluent, could afford to let others work his land. "With or without help, he had to apply his own muscle to agriculture. He could be a gentleman and a farmer, but not a gentleman-farmer."[1]

The colonial officers in London had hoped to import a British gentry into the new colony, to make it a model of the motherland, and to stifle American egalitarianism. They failed. The first settlers, while devoted to the crown, had been raised in American colonies and had inherited their ethos of equality of rights. The thousands who came after them, at first from England and Scotland, then increasingly from Ireland, Germany, and Poland, were fleeing exactly the sorts of regime that the British were trying to impose. Powerful land barons, who might well have formed the nucleus of an Ontario aristocracy, instead found themselves battling on their settlers' behalf before obdurate colonial administrators.

Before long, two social forces competed for control of the colony's political agenda: a British Tory elite that believed Upper Canadian society should be modelled as closely as possible on the aristocratic oligarchy of the mother country, and an independent-minded yeomanry that had no intention of submitting to such a scheme. The Tory aristocracy, whose Toronto leadership was dubbed the Family Compact, initially dominated the political life of the province. But with each passing year the broader population grew more restive. People chafed at the vast amounts of good farmland reserved for the Church of England and at the high tariffs designed to protect the colony's manufacturing industries and provide revenues for the administration. Farmers demanded easy access to American and British markets. Of greatest concern was the matter of representation: although there was a popularly elected Legislative Assembly, the governor often ruled by fiat, with the aid of the Family Compact.

On one occasion this resistance flared into violence. William Lyon Mackenzie, a hot-headed Scots newspaper publisher who became the first of numerous eccentric mayors of Toronto, led an attempted coup in 1837 aimed at toppling the Family Compact. It failed pathetically and two men were hanged, but Mackenzie escaped to the United States. Later he returned, pardoned, to resume his often libelous tirades both inside and outside the Assembly.

Mackenzie's dream of reform was widely shared. The father-and-son team of William and Robert Baldwin fought tenaciously for responsible government, in which the Executive Council, or cabinet, would not only be drawn from but would answer to a democratically elected Legislative Assembly. In 1841 the British attempted to solve Upper Canadian restiveness, and the more serious problem of French resistance to imperial rule in Lower Canada, by uniting the two colonies. To sell the deal, the Colonial Office offered both colonies a limited measure of responsible government. The colonists jumped at the chance, and immediately wrested the powers of patronage and policy from the dismayed governors general.

Despite the blessing of responsible government, the new union proved to be the worst of all possible worlds. The Upper Canadians, whose numbers at the time were smaller than those of Lower Canada, demanded and got equal representation in the legislature. Before long, however, they discovered that their population was growing so rapidly that they would soon be in the majority. Immediately, displaying the righteous self-interest for which they were already becoming famous, they began to press for representation by population ("rep by pop"). The French Canadian majority in Lower Canada resented this attempt by the British and the Canadian English to overwhelm them. They sought survival through an alliance with sympathetic conservatives in Upper Canada, the inheritors of the old Family Compact who abhorred the obstreperous independence of their compatriots. Thereupon the Upper Canadian majority, angered by what they saw as the papist French domination of their affairs, voted for the various factions that had coalesced under the Reform umbrella. With the passing years, as everything seemed to be getting increasingly unstable, people became more and more ill-tempered. Repeated elections failed to produce coalitions that could govern successfully, and intelligent statesmen began searching for alternatives.

It was that search and those alternatives—a new federation or an independent state within or outside the British Empire—that drew the delegates to Toronto in November 1859 to hear the fiery speeches at the Reform convention.

Brown had called the convention for November 9 and 10 in Toronto's St. Lawrence Hall. Hundreds of delegates from across the colony had passed between the classical columns of the monument to Toronto's growing prosperity and prestige on King Street and had squeezed their way into the elegant Great Hall to debate six resolutions that Brown himself had framed with the help of a carefully stacked committee. In the wake of the Macdonald-Cartier "Double Shuffle" that had unseated Brown's brief administration, the Reform leader had decided that a moderate approach had the greatest chance of success. The union needed to be reformed, but preserved. The equal status of Quebec within the Assembly, so galling to Upper Canadians now that their population had surpassed that of the older colony, had to be abolished. In its place, representation by population would give Canada West its rightful share of seats. But a total breach was out of the question. One way or another, Brown was convinced, Upper Canada had to find some means of working with the Lower province. Quebec controlled the St. Lawrence River, and therefore had the power to choke, or at least greatly inconvenience, the centre's thriving economy. Besides, the two colonies had a shared history: they were next-door neighbours, members of the British Empire, and the best defence for each other against the expansionist Americans.

A total split would never sell with the voters. Many would see it as a divorce, not only from Quebec but from the British Empire itself, an act of republicanism or even American annexationism. Apart from a few passionate Clear Grits who called for annexation, such nonsense had no support among electors. The first wave of settlers had come after the revolutionary war as Loyalists, to escape the distasteful new republic of the United States of America. Most of the others had emigrated from England, Scotland, or Ireland. With the exception of the Irish Catholics, their devotion to Queen Victoria was absolute, and anything tainted with even a whiff of disloyalty would spell electoral oblivion

Besides, the Northwest was starting to open up. Only a hundred miles out of Toronto, the traveller crossing the Severn River discovered that the land changed suddenly from rolling farmland to rock-lined lakes. Throughout the endless tracts of forest that gripped the stony soil of the Precambrian Shield, loggers were already hard at work stripping the land of trees for the mills. Farther west, the first few settlers were breaking up the prairie sod and finding it fit for farming, despite the long, cold winters and the short summers. On the West Coast, there was a thriving colony in British Columbia, and reports of gold in the Rocky Mountains. The first dreamers were already talking about a federation of British colonies from the Atlantic to the Pacific, a federation that Upper Canadians expected to control. "The wealth of 400,000 square miles of territory will flow through our waters and be gathered by our merchants, manufacturers and agriculturists," ran an editorial in Brown's *Globe* a few years later. "Our sons will occupy the chief places of this vast territory, we will form its institutions, supply its rulers, teach its schools, fill its stores, run its mills, navigate its streams. Every article of European manufacture, every pound of tropical produce will pass through our stores. Our seminaries of learning will be filled by its people. Our cities will be the centres of its business and education, its health and refinement."[2]

Loyalty to Britain, the dream of a greater federation, and the need to share the Great Lakes–St. Lawrence system with Quebec all pointed to a plan to reshape the union rather than destroy it. The challenge for Reform was to get all the major factions to agree that a revised federation was the best and most realistic option for the party.

The very idea of holding the convention was extraordinary. To gather the leading members of a political movement together, to debate and pass resolutions, to found future party policy on those resolutions, and to affirm the party leader—to hold, in other words, a modern political convention—was unprecedented in the colony, or anywhere in British North America. Brown stage-managed it as carefully as he dared, conspiring with other key men in the wording of the resolutions: that the existing union of French and English Canada imposed by Great Britain in 1841 had failed; that the precedent of requiring double majorities from both Canada East and Canada West in the Assembly before any major legislation could pass had proved unworkable; that the eighteen-year experiment in responsible government, in which the Executive Council answered to the elected legislature rather than the governor general, had not provided efficient and honest administration; and that a federation of all the British North American colonies, including Nova Scotia, New Brunswick, Prince Edward Island, and Newfoundland, was impractical at this time and would delay necessary reforms. The convention was asked to endorse that, "in the opinion of this assembly the best practicable remedy for the evils now encountered in the government of Canada is to be found in the formation of two or more local governments to which shall be committed the control of all matters of a local or sectional character and a general government charged with such matters as are necessarily common to both sections of the province."[3] The general government would be elected on the basis of representation by population.

The 520 delegates began to debate these resolutions on the first day of the convention, taking matters up again the next morning. At first things went well, as speaker after speaker rose to support a proposed federation. All was unfolding just as Brown and his allies had hoped until George Sheppard asked for a chance to speak. In a way, Brown had himself to blame for the intervention. He had brought the English firebrand onto the editorial staff of the *Globe* only the year before, to help write editorials while he wallowed in the gloom of his Double Shuffle defeat. Sheppard went much further than Brown had been prepared to go, demanding "radical organic changes" to the union government. Indeed, in a powerful series of editorials only six months before the convention, Sheppard had pushed the *Globe* into demanding the complete dissolution of the union and the inauguration of an American-style government with a written constitution and an executive separate from, but dependent on, the legislature. By July the *Globe* was envisioning three separate British North American states, each with its own tie to the empire. As Brown regained his vigour and began organizing the convention for November, he reined in Sheppard's diatribes, but he couldn't control Sheppard himself. The disgruntled editorialist rose to demand that the convention consider not federation, but separation. "I appear here as the advocate of simple, unadulterated dissolution of the union!" he told the delegates.[4]

Negotiating a federal union would take years, probably fail, and, in the meantime, leave Ontario captive to Quebec. It would require the expensive trappings of a vice-regal head of state. Most important, Sheppard found it highly unlikely that any federation could be formed that would respect the rights and powers of the individual colonies. "I do not think you can find any union of the colonies based on the federated principle," he warned the assembly. The Americans to the south appeared determined to tear their republic apart over exactly that refusal by the central government to accept the rights of the southern states to practise their peculiar institution of slavery.

Cries of support from dissolutionists rang out around the room. Sheppard moved to amend the motion on federation, calling for "totally unqualified dissolution." Defenders of both sides began arguing forcefully. As the speeches dragged on for hours, it increasingly appeared that the convention could split, with the Reform cause once again betrayed by internal dissent.

The federalists countered with an amendment of their own, a compromise that would strike the term "general government" out of the key resolution, replacing it with the vague phrase "some joint authority." Surely even the most ardent dissenters were not opposed to a coordinating body to supervise matters of common interest between Lower and Upper Canada, they argued. This plea prompted a fresh round of speeches, as the day waned and night fell, until, finally, through sheer exhaustion, there was nothing left to say.

Now was the time for Brown. He had sat out the day, listening quietly, waiting for the arguments to run their course. By common, unspoken consent, he rose to conclude the debate. In tense silence, the tall, stern, white-haired leader strode through the quietened hall and mounted the stage. His own future, the future of Upper Canada's most important party, and perhaps even the future of the colony itself rested on this moment. Upper Canada had reached a fork. The convention was going to decide which path to take: to a new federation with Lower Canada and possibly beyond, or to independence. And every one of those delegates believed that independence might be inevitable, whether they supported the notion or not.

Though Brown was famed as an orator, he often displayed an awkward diffidence at the beginning of his speeches, mumbling through his opening remarks and gaining momentum only as he bit into the meat of his message. The delegates waited patiently as their leader congratulated the organizers of the conference on their fine efforts and praised the many speech-makers on their wisdom. But soon he came to the heart of the matter: which was it to be, dissolution or federation? Which destiny would Reformers push the colony towards? His voice strengthening in conviction, he argued for federation.

Brown quickly granted that dissolution might be the best solution for Upper Canada, in theory. "I have no morbid terror of dissolution," he maintained. "I have no fear that the people of Upper Canada would ever desire to become the fag end of the neighbouring republic!"[5] An independent Upper Canada would remain faithful to the crown and free of both French and American domination.

But was it practical? The seasoned political veterans in the Legislative Assembly, he reminded them, knew in their hearts it was not. "There are many members of the legislature here tonight, who speak from the field of battle, who thoroughly understand the materials of which the legislature is composed. And there is not one of them who will not tell you that it would be cause for deep regret were this convention to declare for entire dissolution of the union."[6] There simply wasn't sufficient support in all parts of the province, he argued, especially in the eastern counties, for a total separation and an independent path.

Besides, what was the real root of their grievances? Domination by Canada East. A lack of real representation in the legislature. Unpopular policies foisted on the people against their will. Corrupt and inefficient governments. Would not federation remove all these obstacles by separating the two colonies, while providing a loose confederation in which they could cooperate in matters of mutual interest? Besides, if one colony went it alone, surely the other would as well. "Are you content to hand over the entire control of the St. Lawrence, to have custom-house officers stopping our railroad cars and our steamers at certain points in their downward journey and overhauling all the passengers as if entering a foreign country?"[7] No appeal to an Upper Canadian was as convincing as the appeal to commercial self-interest.

But Brown could appeal to hearts as well as heads. Who in that hall did not dream of a greater future for all British North America? How would dissolution, as opposed to federation, aid that goal? "I do hope there is not one Canadian in this assembly who does not look forward with high hopes to the day when these northern countries shall stand out among the nations of the world as one great confederation! ... Is it not clear that the former [dissolution] would be a death blow to the hopes of future union, while the latter [federation] may at some future day readily furnish the machinery of a great confederation?"[8]

That sealed it. The delegates roared with approval: federation it would be. No tariffs, control of internal affairs, and a great confederacy stretching one day from sea to sea. They would be at the centre of it all. Sheppard withdrew his proposed amendment. The amended motion carried unanimously and the convention dissolved, united and determined.

The convention of 1859 stands as one of the seminal moments in the history of Ontario and the drive towards Confederation. It settled the issue of dissolution versus federation in Upper Canada's largest party, uniting it behind both the policy and the leadership of George Brown. However much the wily John A. Macdonald, English leader of the existing union, might resist a new federation, however much he might prefer the status quo of a united colony with power brokered by coalitions of east and west, the push towards federation was now inevitable. Five years later, Macdonald would exploit its political possibilities with an acumen Brown could never master and capture the movement for himself, stage-managing the deal at Charlottetown that would lead to the creation of the Dominion of Canada.

But the Confederation of 1867 would be as much a divorce as a union. It would sunder Canada West from Canada East, severing the unworkable arrangement under which the colonies had struggled for more than two decades. It was the vehicle by which Upper Canadians would acquire complete control over their internal affairs, without retaliation from that other large colony downriver. It laid the foundation for what the colony's leaders saw as a greater continental federation dominated by Ontario.

There was no doubt in the minds of the Reformers that November night about the nature of the federation. It would be just that: a loose linking of colonies sovereign within their own sphere, cooperating on matters of mutual interest through a central government—

"some joint authority"—that served their needs. Pragmatic, self-centred, the tinge of superiority cloaked in the rhetoric of empire—this was George Brown's Confederation. It was not the only vision, and it would even cease to be Brown's once he became mired in the negotiations at Charlottetown and Quebec. But it was what the leaders who were closest to the majority of the people wanted that night as they crowded into the St. Lawrence Hall. It was how Confederation would evolve, at least in its initial decades.

It is what Confederation is turning back to today.

2

Macdonald's Bane

By 1864, five years after Reform's landmark convention, the Province of Canada had become utterly ungovernable. Political leaders spent weeks trying to cobble together coalitions of Lower and Upper Canadian legislators, lost more weeks defending their shaky coalitions in the legislature, and then promptly went down to defeat on non-confidence motions. In the previous two years there had been four administrations, partly because the modern party system had not yet been fully formed and individual legislators thought nothing of voting with the government on one measure and against it on another, but mostly because the union was a failure at heart. Neither Canada East nor Canada West wanted to belong to each other: one was French, Catholic, deeply rooted in its history, and painfully conscious of its lost ascendancy; the other was English, Protestant, aggressively expansionist, and optimistic about its future. It was time for a separation.

But not time for a divorce. Both colonies recognized that, alone, they risked being absorbed by their dangerous neighbour to the south. The Civil War, far from enfeebling the divided and distracted American republic, had transformed it. By 1864 the American federal government had a million men in uniform; its industries had leapt forward in size and sophistication, supplying the great war machine. The American colossus was emerging from the war more powerful, more militant, and more expansionist than ever in its history. Where would it turn its attention when the war ended—west or north? This was no time to disband the already vulnerable Canadian union. Besides, like any couple, the two colonies had grown used to each other. Neither wanted to sleep in the same bed, but that didn't mean they couldn't share the house. No one among the merchant class wanted the tolls, tariffs, and other impediments to trade that the total separation of the two might entail. Some new kind of federation was needed. Moreover, the question of how to settle the former lands of the Hudson's Bay Company in the northwest, as well as the province of British Columbia on the Pacific, remained unresolved, even as the Canadas bickered. Although Canada West increased in population and prosperity despite the political paralysis, observers agreed that the colony would grow even faster if it received the benefit of actual government now and then.

Everyone understood a simple truth: if the existing legislature were dissolved and a new federation created, it would be an act of partition, not union. A new federation would dissolve the Province of Canada, substituting instead a loose coordinating body to address items of mutual concern, leaving the two communities free to pursue their separate destinies. George Brown had this notion in mind when, on May 16, 1864, he rose in the legislature in Quebec City—one of the rotating capitals, with Toronto, of this dysfunctional union—to propose the creation of a "constitutional committee" to explore changes to the existing union. "I simply ask the House to say that a great evil exists, that a remedy must be found, and to appoint a committee to consider what that remedy should be," he told his troubled colleagues.[1]

Even Brown's bitter political foes John A. Macdonald and George-Étienne Cartier, who had thrived on the bartering and brokering of the union coalition, wearily agreed that the situation had become impossible. They joined the committee, which achieved little beyond agreeing that "a strong feeling was found to exist among members of the committee in favour of changes in the direction of a federative system, applied either to Canada alone or to the whole British North American provinces."[2] Macdonald ultimately voted against even this generalization. But when his next attempt at a coalition went down to defeat that June, he and Cartier accepted Brown's overture to form "a Great Coalition," under the titular leadership of Sir Étienne Taché, pledged to as-yet-undefined constitutional change. The honourable members watched in amazement as Brown crossed the floor to join Macdonald in a united administration dedicated to the single goal of dismantling the union it governed.

Happily, the colonies of Nova Scotia, New Brunswick, and Prince Edward Island were also examining the possibility of an Atlantic federation. They had agreed to meet in Charlottetown on August 31. When the leaders of the coalition asked if a Canadian delegation might attend the talks, the Maritimers agreed. On September 1, 1864, the steamship *Queen Victoria*, carrying Macdonald, Brown, and other leaders from the Province of Canada, arrived at Charlottetown. They found the people there greatly excited over the arrival of a circus, the first in twenty years, complete with elephants.

Perhaps it was the circus, the fine late-summer weather, or the pastoral enchantments of Prince Edward Island—"as pretty a country as you could ever put your eye upon,"[3] Brown called it—but an air of optimism and good cheer pervaded the seven days of deliberations. Champagne helped. Local dignitaries went out of their way to host elaborate dinners and soporific lunches. On the second day, for example, the conference having adjourned at three o'clock, the delegates were treated to a luncheon of lobsters, oysters, and champagne. Even the serious Brown confessed in a letter to his wife that "this killed the day, and we spent the beautiful moonlight evening in walking, talking, or boating, as the mood was on us."[4]

Nonetheless, the twenty-three delegates worked hard, clustered around the long table in the conference room of Province House, considering proposals, debating principles, nitpicking details. Almost immediately, the original intent of the conference—to discuss the possible union of Nova Scotia, New Brunswick, and Prince Edward Island—was forgotten, as the Maritime delegates listened with fascination to their Canadian counterparts' offer: one strong, sovereign central government for all of British North America, but with the local powers of the original provinces protected and assured. Intoxicated by the fragrant island air, or just intoxicated, the delegates warmed to the contagious notion of forging a new nation. "Champagne and union" became the twin themes; by the end of the seventh day, the delegates unanimously affirmed their willingness, in principle, to negotiate a possible union of the British North American colonies.

The delegates met again a month later in the snow and rain of a wet Quebec City autumn, the summer luncheons giving way to glittering balls that lasted till 3 a.m. Amid an unceasing social whirl of parties, receptions, and too little sleep, the delegates somehow summoned the strength to negotiate the details of what would become Canada's constitution. That constitution would centre on a powerful federal government, responsible not only for customs, defence, and finances but for any other residual responsibilities not specifically assigned to the provincial government. Even Brown, who five years before had envisioned a central government so weak it would serve only as a clearing-house for matters of joint provincial concern, now enthusiastically supported an agreement so centralizing in its principles that the provincial parliaments' work would be "largely clerical and routine," presided over by watchful lieutenant-governors who would "bring these bodies into harmony with the general government."[5] Three years later, after much to-ing and fro-ing by the Atlantic provinces in which Prince Edward Island and Newfoundland elected to reject the proposed Confederation, the British Parliament passed the British North America Act into law, and Canada was born. The new dominion, in the eyes of almost all observers, boasted a central government only a shade shy of the full legislative union of Great Britain, with the provincial governments reduced, in the eyes of Brown and the other fathers, to the status of "mere municipal institutions."[6] George Brown appeared to have betrayed every principle he had embraced at the St. Lawrence Hall convention of 1859. He had transformed "some joint authority" into Leviathan. Why?

The simplest and most powerful reason lay south of the border. Since the St. Lawrence Hall meeting, Canadians had watched in fascinated horror as the United States consumed itself in four years of civil war, a war that would kill 625,000 men in uniform, more than the total of all American battlefield deaths in wars since then. As they watched the conflict, British North American politicians became convinced that the war was the fault of a constitution in which the powers of the federal government had been left too weak and defused, instilling in the states pretensions of grandeur. "The fatal error which they have committed," Macdonald argued, "... was in giving to each a distinct sovereignty, in giving each a distinct sovereign power except in those instances where they were specially reserved by the constitution and conferred upon the General Government."[7] If it had been left to Macdonald, the new union would have abolished the provincial governments entirely.

The most able politician in all British North America, Macdonald had flourished under the original union government and saw no reason why the new federation shouldn't simply expand and increase the power of the existing legislature. But he also knew that he hadn't a hope of carrying the idea of full legislative amalgamation. Quebec had resisted union with Canada West; it would never agree to being further submerged in the English sea by a legislative union with the Atlantic colonies as well. His own Upper Canadian allies would also have deserted him; George Brown had entered the coalition only to sever the existing union; he would never agree to a new all-powerful one. Furthermore, the leaders of the Atlantic colonies had not the slightest wish to be swallowed up by their larger counterparts to the west.

So a federation it would have to be. But Macdonald, who had quickly become the most senior negotiator at the conference by virtue of his clear intelligence, masterful political skills, and ties to both the Quebec *bleus* and the Upper Canadian conservatives, was determined to make the federation the most strongly centralist one possible. To that end, he persuaded the delegates, including Brown, to support a parcel of centralist principles. First, unlike the Americans, the Canadians would vest the central government with "residual powers": any authority not specifically defined as belonging to the provinces would reside with the central government. Second, the central government would have one enormous club: it could veto, or "disallow," any legislation passed by a provincial government within one year of its passage. Third, the central government would be given what were seen as all "the great powers"—trade and commerce, finance, foreign affairs, as well as "all matters of a general character"—and could make laws "for the peace, welfare and good government of the federated provinces," which meant it could legislate on just about anything. Fourth, the federal government would have access to all the major sources of revenue, especially the revenues from tariffs, while the provinces would largely be dependent on federal grants, unless they wanted to enter the politically explosive realm of income taxes (the mere thought of which caused most nineteenth-century politicians to swoon). Finally, the lieutenant-governors of the provinces would be appointed by the federal government and be subordinate to the governor general. Macdonald intended to make lieutenant-governors, in effect, agents of the federal government, liaising with the provincial powers and ensuring that their policies remained secondary to, and in harmony with, the federal power.

Surprisingly, Brown, along with the other delegates in Upper Canada, Quebec, Nova Scotia, and New Brunswick, agreed to all these measures. Why? Beyond the sobering effect of the American example and the machinations of Macdonald, sheer momentum had something to do with it. The Fathers felt themselves to be part of a great nation-building exercise; they knew they were crafting history. No one wanted to be the rock on which Confederation foundered. And Brown had his own particular reasons for conversion. The whole Reform movement was based on the principle of representation by population. The House of Commons, where true power would reside (the Fathers realized that the many compromises involved in creating the Senate had rendered it useless), would be elected through rep by pop. Ontario would have nearly half the seats in the House, Brown reasoned, ensuring that its interests would be well represented. Furthermore, although the provincial powers would be limited, they would not be insignificant. Section 92 of the British North America Act, which mirrored the Quebec Conference agreement, gave the provinces power over natural resources, public works, "property and civil rights in the province," the administration of justice, prisons, education, and "generally all matters of a merely local and private nature." These were substantial powers. Brown actually argued at Quebec that the provinces had been given too much.

Then there were issues of instinct. Brown held a deep-seated suspicion of Quebec and everything in it. He found the union intolerable: his colony's English, Protestant destiny contaminated by Popish French plots; Catholic schools infiltrating the education system; and French *bleus* dominating the governing coalitions. He was, frankly, racist towards the French—a not uncommon sentiment at the time, or even later. Confederation, in limiting all provincial powers, would limit Quebec as well, binding it within a union of English provinces and diminishing its influence.

In the end, Brown was co-opted by his sense of history. Caught up in the excitement of the process, keenly aware that he was helping to give birth to a new country—one that might one day border three oceans—and beguiled once again by the force of Macdonald's elegant logic and power to persuade, Brown put behind him the resolutions of 1859 and the promise to limit the general government to some joint authority. He was swept away. "All right!!!" an ecstatic Brown wrote to his wife on November 6, the evening the proposed constitution was signed. "Conference through at six o'clock this evening—constitution adopted—a most creditable document—a complete reform of all the abuses and injustice we have complained of! Is it not wonderful? French Canadianism entirely extinguished! ... Hurrah!"[8]

From the moment the Confederation document was signed in Quebec City, Brown's influence was in eclipse. Even before the new nation was born, he had resigned from the government and returned to the *Globe*. The leadership of the emerging Liberal Party passed on to new hands and, when Brown failed to win his own southern Ontario riding in the inaugural elections of 1867, he gave up his political career and concerned himself with his expanding newspaper, his farming interests, and his deteriorating finances. His career was largely over and his legacy established when, on March 20, 1880, he got into an argument with a disgruntled former employee who pulled out a gun and, in the ensuing tussle, shot the publisher in the leg. The wound became infected and seven weeks later, Brown was dead.

Brown may have appeared stern and intransigent, but at heart he was an idealist, a democrat whose passions sometimes clouded his reason, permitting him to be manipulated by his more calculating political enemies. He was, nonetheless, in many ways the founder of Ontario and the co-founder of Confederation. His single-minded determination to create a federation that protected Ontario's interests by embracing the democratic principle of representation by population compelled the political leadership of the old union to come to a table he had crafted, even if, in the end, they succeeded in pushing him away from the meal. There would not have been a

Canada or an Ontario—at least as we know it today—without George Brown.

For these reasons, despite all his failures, Brown is much better known than Oliver Mowat, his successor. Yet if Brown's popularity in the history books is deserved, Mowat's obscurity is unfair. Brown helped to give birth to Ontario, but Mowat shaped and defined it, forging in the face of fierce federal opposition the physical and political entity that dominates the Confederation today. Brown, the romantic, was doomed to repeated political defeat; Mowat, the pragmatist, never took on a major battle that he lost. Oliver Mowat was the most successful premier in Ontario's history and, far more than George Brown, he deserves to be remembered as its most passionate advocate.

Mowat had come to the Quebec Conference as part of the Brown delegation, the senior lieutenant of the Reform chieftain. Quiet, sober (literally—he was a teetotaller), precise, short-sighted and mutton-chopped, rather dull, Mowat appeared the opposite of both the righteous Brown and the cheerfully Machiavellian Macdonald. Both had served as his mentors. Mowat was a Kingston-based Scot, like Macdonald; they attended the same school, and Mowat got his legal start in Macdonald's law office. The two had even considered going into partnership and, as Mowat's biographer observed, "a firm combining the dashing charm of Macdonald and the utter respectability of Mowat might have been a tremendous success."[9]

But both men had political ambitions, and someone had actually to practise law, so they went their separate ways. Mowat's path led him to Toronto, to the obscure but highly profitable realm of chancery law, and then into politics—as a Reformer, to Macdonald's chagrin. Relations went steadily downhill from there. Mowat had already displayed considerable intelligence and competence during a brief stint as minister in one of the many shifting coalition governments of the time, and he was now considered George Brown's second-in-command. At the conference, the key task of introducing and helping to describe the list of powers assigned to the central and provincial governments fell to Mowat.

It was clear during the debates that Mowat was not entirely in accord with Brown. Although he followed his political leader in supporting the strongly centralist proposed constitution, Mowat openly disagreed with him over the then crucial role of agriculture, which Brown—by now a thoroughly committed centralist—thought should be an exclusively federal responsibility. Mowat argued that agriculture was also a provincial concern, and that responsibility should be jointly shared. Mowat's position carried the day, although he was defeated in his attempts to convince the delegates to provide for an elected upper chamber, which would have made it more powerful than the appointed one.

But Mowat did accept—indeed, he helped to formulate—the division of powers within Confederation that appeared to ensure a powerful central government. While his reasoning was never recorded, the accomplished lawyer probably grasped the true implications of the new constitution better than its other drafters. The British North America Act first and foremost ensured that the provincial governments would be responsible: that is, they would be democratic, answerable only to their electors, and in full authority in the areas over which they had jurisdiction. And those jurisdictions were more formidable than they at first appeared to be, encompassing health, education, and charities—which would later expand to the enormous category of social services—as well as control over crown lands and the resources that would be extracted from them. The provincial governments could levy direct taxes; they had authority over municipal governments, the police, and the administration of justice; and they were the guardians of civil and property rights. There was nothing feeble about that. As for much of the rest, including the subordinate role of the lieutenant-governor, the wording was unclear: it could be argued either way. And Mowat was a better lawyer than Macdonald.

Mowat and other delegates, in fact, envisioned the central government as anything but dominant. Mowat later insisted—perhaps indulging in a bit of historical revisionism—that the Fathers saw Confederation as nothing more than the transference of the imperial government from Westminster to Parliament Hill. The imperial government had the power of disallowance, but that had been used only once in the past twenty-five years. It had also appointed the governors general, but these nominal heads of administration had become increasingly impotent as representative government became more entrenched. The colonies were already largely self-governing; they would remain so, with Ottawa rather than London playing the role of benevolent but by no means domineering matron. As historian Christopher Moore observes:

> If there was a Machiavellian brilliance in Oliver Mowat's work at Quebec, it lay in perceiving that what had reduced London's Imperial power to ceremonial trappings ... would just as efficiently undermine the powers Ottawa might one day claim to find in the Quebec resolutions. If the provinces were responsible governments answerable to their own electorates, Ottawa would find itself unable to interfere with them in their allocated spheres, just as London had already done.[10]

Of course, the federal government, unlike the Colonial Office, would also be directly elected. The contest, then, might shape up as one both of constitutional law and of governments competing for the hearts of the voters. If so, Mowat appeared serene at the prospect of the outcome.

Macdonald, for all his bluster about the power of the central government, may have seen what Mowat saw and recognized in his former student a potentially dangerous political foe. The Quebec

Conference was still in mid-deliberation when Macdonald, as the attorney general for Canada West, offered to make his erstwhile protégé a judge in the Chancery Court. There were only three seats on the Chancery bench, all of them life appointments, and the temptation for Mowat was irresistible. He accepted immediately and ceased all political activity. With his dangerous rival safely dispatched—permanently, it seemed—Macdonald convinced the union legislature to approve the Quebec Resolutions, and Westminster to do its duty. A grateful embryonic nation made Sir John A. Macdonald its first prime minister. He immediately began manipulating both the constitution and the political landscape to increase the power of Ottawa and emasculate the provincial capitals.

Whatever formal powers the British North America Act might confer, Macdonald understood that precedent and practice would truly decide who did what in the new country. Canada's first prime minister was determined to ensure that Ottawa would do as much, and the political capitals as little, as the law allowed.

First and foremost, he needed a friendly government in Ontario. George Brown, displaying his typical political acumen, quickly found himself on the sidelines, as Macdonald helped John Sandfield Macdonald, once a moderate Reformer, now a moderate Conservative, to form the first crucial provincial government. Sandfield Macdonald promptly allied himself with the federal chieftain and began to wield the potent political weapon of patronage. In the nineteenth century, far more than today, the secret to political success lay largely in controlling and exploiting the powers of government largesse. It was considered entirely proper for postmasters, liquor inspectors, customs officials—virtually everyone who drew a government paycheque—to earn that position as a reward for loyalty to a political master. Competence was expected, and overt corruption as frowned upon then as now, but it didn't take the highest level of skill to issue a liquor licence, and the issuer might as well be one whose extracurricular activities were in aid of the governing party. Sir John A. was an unsurpassed master at the art of granting favours and collecting debts, and Ontario's first premier did his best to follow suit. The new province required new institutions, and Sandfield Macdonald was determined to see them located in ridings whose electors showed discernment in voting. He once dismissed a group of delegates from the Liberal stronghold of Strathroy with the question, "What the hell has Strathroy done for me?"[11]

Most important for Sir John A., Sandfield Macdonald was loyal. Canada's first prime minister was well aware of the ambiguities in the wording of the British North America Act and the vital role that precedent would play in establishing conventions. The prime minister hoped that the provisions of the act, coupled with an aggressive and confident central government and subservient local ones, would one day bring about the legislative union to which he had originally aspired. He fully expected, within a few years, that the provincial governments would be "absorbed in the General Power." In the meantime, they should be treated as nothing more than trumped-up municipal governments. "My own opinion," he proclaimed, "is that the General Government or Parliament should pay no more regard to the status or position of the Local Governments than they would to the prospects of the ruling party in the corporation of Quebec or Montreal."[12]

To ensure that the provincial governments began life enfeebled and remained that way, it was vital that the premier of the most powerful province be cooperative. Sandfield Macdonald could, on occasion, act of his own volition; we owe him, for example, the creation of the comprehensive public school system advocated by Egerton Ryerson. But he believed that government in Ontario and Canada would mature only when the quarrelsome, independent-minded backbenchers who made and broke the many coalitions of the past were replaced by disciplined, powerful political parties. He worked hard, and largely successfully, to mould the Conservative version of that party in Ontario, but to do so he needed the full support of the federal Conservative leaders, especially in the realm of patronage appointments. Both the Macdonalds agreed that mutual cooperation was in the best interests of their party, and they cooperated handsomely.

Despite the reluctance Westminster had shown earlier to disallow legislation, Sir John was determined to wield the power early and often. What better way to establish his authority than to remind the provinces that any legislation provoking Ottawa's displeasure would be swiftly and certainly negated? During his first term in power, the prime minister disallowed or instructed lieutenant-governors to withhold royal assent to twenty-two provincial bills, from an act to empower the police courts of Halifax to sentence young offenders to attend industrial schools to an act to incorporate the Manitoba Railways Co. The exception was Ontario. During Sandfield Macdonald's four years in office, the Ontario legislature found itself subject to federal disallowance only twice. The reason, simply, was that the lesser Macdonald was so accommodating. The two corresponded frequently, with the Ontario premier regularly submitting proposed legislation to the prime minister for his comments. Often the prime minister would recommend changes; sometimes the premier would resist the recommendations. On the whole, however, the relationship was close and the roles clearly defined: a prime minister's dream of executive federalism come true.

Despite Sandfield Macdonald's best efforts to forge his ragtag coalition of moderate Reformers and Conservatives into a disciplined political party, he remained vulnerable to the obstinacy and opportunism of its members, and by 1871 it was clear the government was finished. It didn't help that his own finance minister resigned and crossed the floor to the opposition. The Patent Combination, as Sandfield Macdonald's conservative coalition was called, suffered from the usual accusations of corruption and incompetence, but it also suffered from its too convivial ties with the Conservatives in Ottawa. The bloom of the Confederation rose had quickly withered.

The cheering for the new dominion had scarcely subsided before the sober reality of what had been given away began to be comprehended by the new province's political elites. Ontario, they concluded, had been snookered. The first hint came when the federal government, under pressure to keep a reluctant Nova Scotia from withdrawing from Confederation, unilaterally revised the grant allocations, improving the federal stipend to the reluctant province. Since most dominion revenues came from tariffs and other sources generated by Ontario's economic activity, Grit politicians there denounced the federal Tory move as a ploy to buy the poorer province's loyalty to the federal government, with Ontario providing the silver. George Brown, now safely back at the *Globe* and possessed of a blissfully short memory, thundered that the Confederation deal was a disaster for the province and needed to be revised.

The Red River Rebellion only worsened matters for Sandfield Macdonald. Protestant Ontario baulked at the federal government's willingness to recognize the Métis uprising of Louis Riel by establishing the province of Manitoba in 1870. There was more than sheer bigotry to their rants; many Ontarians—correctly, as it turned out—suspected that the federal government hoped to use the Riel crisis to create a large new province on Ontario's northwest, cheating it of its imperial destiny to dominate the former Hudson's Bay Company lands.

Ontario, unlike any other province in Confederation, was both a frontier and an imperial culture, founded on assumptions of progress, expansion, and power. While Quebec brooded over its lost nationhood, and the Atlantic colonies struggled to come to terms with the reality of their economic eclipse, Ontario exulted in its wealth—generated, its citizens had not the slightest doubt, through their own virtue and industriousness—and dreamed of a glorious future. That this future could be truncated by having the northern and western territories annexed to a province fabricated by Ottawa to limit Ontario ambitions was intolerable. As Sid Noel argued in his political history of nineteenth-century Ontario:

> Ontario's fierce determination to expand its territory had not sprung purely, and perhaps not even mainly, from economic motives; it had sprung also from an abiding and at times obsessive concern over status ... Expansion was thus a matter of Upper Canadian pride (or, from other points of view, of Upper Canadian arrogance). Historically, it reflected the same peculiar assumption of entitlement that had been built into the Upper Canadian outlook from the very beginning; for, it must be remembered, land had been the original loyalist imperative, its grant from the Crown the symbolic confirmation of rightness and worth, of political vindication. With astounding fidelity that outlook had been passed on to late-Victorian Ontario, where, after the passage of a century, land remained a potent symbol and was still pursued with a visceral acquisitiveness.[13]

Turbulent changes under way within the Ontario economy and culture in the 1870s and 1880s only sharpened Ontarians' determination to control the lands of the northwest. The easy affluence of Ontario's wheat-based economy was fast disappearing, the victim of changing markets and an end to reciprocity (free trade) with the United States. These changes threw all of Canada into a prolonged recession. Ontario fared far better than the other provinces, whose farmlands were less fertile and whose economies were less able to adjust to change. Although Ontario farmers struggled, and many marginal farms on stony soils failed, the best of them adapted, changing to barley (American breweries loved Ontario barley), dairy, or even rye (for the fast-expanding distilling industry).

The Industrial Revolution had also reached Ontario. The sons and daughters of farmers increasingly abandoned the homestead and headed to Toronto, Hamilton, or Ottawa, where there were jobs in the new factories and mills—even if the cramped rowhouses, lack of water or sewage, and dreary working conditions turned life to grey. Toronto had reached a population of 50,000 (still less than half that of Montreal), and several smaller cities—London, Hamilton, Kingston, Ottawa—increasingly dominated the countryside around them. In eastern Ontario and the Canadian Shield lands north of the lower Severn River, a thriving lumber industry stripped the rocky terrain of its white pine and anything else that was harvestable. The workers lived in rough winter shanties, drinking and fighting, and risked their lives as they floated their logs in booms down the Ottawa River to market. In the spring, they returned to their scrabbly farms.

Irish Catholics were plentiful in the bush, but elsewhere in the province a rigid Protestantism, celebrated and defended by the Orange Order—a narrow-minded anti-Catholic and royalist association brought over by northern Irish immigrants—dominated the religious and political life of the province. Supporters marched defiantly through the Catholic parts of town on the Glorious Twelfth—the anniversary of the Battle of the Boyne, July 12, 1690, when the Protestant William of Orange defeated the Catholic James II. On such days, rum and tempers brought on fierce fist-fights, ending with hangovers and bruises all around.

The restless, aggressive citizens of new-born Ontario* expected both the federal and the provincial government to protect their interests. Instead, Ottawa appeared increasingly intent on placating the Catholics in Quebec and Confederation's poor cousins on the Atlantic, while circumscribing Ontario's manifest westward destiny with a new province in the northwest. Sandfield Macdonald, though

* The new province was initially to be named Toronto, to match the symmetry of Quebec City and Quebec. But resentment of the city's dominance had already reached such a pitch that Westminster heeded a suggestion to name the province after the Great Lake instead.

well aware of the growing anger with Ottawa's imperiousness, was too closely tied to the Conservatives and to Macdonald personally to disavow its policies. His coalition crumbling, his support waning, his health broken, he was forced out of office in 1871 by the Grit leader, Edward Blake, who had been haranguing both the Macdonalds on the abuse of Ontario's rights by the federal government.

While in opposition, Blake had introduced a motion that served as a template for what came to be known as the "compact theory" of Confederation. The federation, Blake argued, was an agreement among the provinces and existed at their sufferance. But John A. Macdonald was abusing that compact by attempting to use the federal power to oppress Ontario and favour other provinces, especially Nova Scotia. No changes to the terms of Confederation, including compensation, he argued, could be made without the unanimous consent of the provinces. Furthermore, the cozy cooperation of the federal and Ontario governments in administering affairs of state was detrimental to both the provincial government and the interests of its citizens. "There should exist no other attitude on the part of the Provincial Government towards the Government of the Dominion than one of neutrality," he said, adding: "that each Government should be absolutely independent of the other in the management of its own affairs."[14] If the provincial government felt that the federal government was acting in a way that contradicted its best interests, he continued, "it becomes the duty of the Province to act ... in order to prevent the infringement of the Provincial interests, of which we believe ourselves to be the guardians."[15]

Blake could have become a powerful advocate of provincial rights, but he had little chance to play the role. In 1872 new legislation wisely prohibited politicians from sitting in both the provincial and the dominion legislatures. When Blake chose the Big Show, and gave up his seat in the provincial legislature, the newly elected Liberal government was suddenly without a leader. The party brass needed a capable and convincing politician able to head up their own still-shaky coalition of Grits and Reformers. Brown's time had passed. But Brown's lieutenant, Oliver Mowat, was available—if he could be persuaded to leave the bench. As it turned out, Mowat was easily persuaded. The leisurely Chancery Court had exhausted its charm, and the devoutly Christian judge still harboured a yen for the rough-house world of politicians.

On October 25, 1872, Mowat was sworn in as premier of Ontario. He served for an unmatched twenty-four years, forged the modern Ontario Liberal Party, transformed the province, and became John A. Macdonald's implacable enemy in a series of escalating battles that reshaped the Confederation. Macdonald raged against his priggish nemesis: "with his little soul rattling like a dried pea in a too large pod—what does he care if he wrecks Confederation?"[16] But the rage was fruitless. Macdonald may have had better biographers, but, as their battles revealed, Mowat was the better politician.

From the beginning the tone was chilly. When Macdonald congratulated Mowat in 1872 on assuming the premiership, he wrote not as a former friend and mentor, but as a wary politician hoping to co-opt, or a least contain, a potential rival. He hoped "the relations between the Dominion government and that of Ontario will be pleasant," he said. "... We all profess to have and I have no doubt sincerely have, the same object in view, the good of the country. We must therefore try to work the new machine ... with as little friction as possible." Mowat responded guardedly: "I have ever felt greatly interested in the success of Confederation, and I agree with you that its success will be aided by proper relations being maintained between the Dominion and Local Governments."[17]

The letters were barely filed before the two began to tussle. It started small, in a skirmish over queen's counsels. Both the federal government, through the governor general, and the provincial governments, through the lieutenant-governors, claimed the right to appoint QCs (in essence, rewards to lawyers for good and faithful service to the party). Since naming QCs was an instrument of patronage, and patronage was all-important in nineteenth-century politics, the matter generated some heat. Macdonald tried to dispose of the issue by writing to Mowat confidentially, asserting that although the governor general had the formal right to make the appointments, he saw no reason why provincial governments could not pass legislation empowering their lieutenants-governors to name QCs as well. Mowat did precisely that, yet his legislation made it clear that the Ontario government was not conferring on the lieutenant-governor the right to name QCs, but affirming a right that already existed—a seemingly obscure point that would become amplified with each future clash.

Within two years Mowat had introduced another bill, affirming that escheats—estates whose proceeds revert to the crown because their owners died without leaving a will—would be acquired by the provincial government. Macdonald, at the time, was offstage, swept to defeat in 1873 over the Pacific Scandal. (The scandal revealed that even in Victorian Canada there were limits to the abuses of patronage. A telegram had become public in which Macdonald had implored the head of the syndicate proposing to build the Canadian Pacific Railway to send more money to help finance the Conservative Party campaign. The resulting scandal brought down the government.) But even the sympathetic Liberal administration of Alexander Mackenzie was not prepared to see provincial governments acquire such powers, and it disallowed the bill. Mowat's response was powerful and prophetic. The rights of the crown had existed separately in each individual colony before Confederation, he replied, and the same relationship with the crown existed after Confederation as before. The implications were profound: Mowat was arguing that sovereignty, the affirmation of a political community's independence, resided not only with the crown in Parliament—with the governor general and the federal government—but equally with the crown in the provincial legislatures, with the lieutenant-governors and the provincial governments. Each level of government, then, would be sovereign, or independent, in the area of its jurisdiction, with neither level senior to the other. Télesphore Fournier, the federal minister of justice, rejected the Ontario position. The lieutenant-governors held no direct commission from the crown, he argued, but derived their authority from the governor general and the federal government. Sovereignty, in other words, stopped at Ottawa.

In the midst of the debate, Edward Blake became federal minister of justice and proposed a most excellent compromise. The question of who should obtain forfeitures—property forfeited as a result of crime—was also in dispute. Since the federal government dealt with the criminal law, and the provinces with the administration of justice, Blake proposed that the provinces be responsible for escheats, and the federal government for forfeitures. When a Quebec court awarded an escheat to the provincial government, the case appeared to be closed, and Mowat accepted the compromise.

But a far more visceral issue was pushing itself to the surface. The northwest boundary had still not been settled. The Macdonald government had proposed a northern boundary that would have begun slightly east of Port Arthur and Fort William (modern Thunder Bay), then stretched along the height of land separating the Hudson Bay and Great Lakes watersheds—essentially a line running east and south. Everything to the north and west would be given to the new province of Manitoba. This was an appalling prospect for the government and population of Ontario. The woods and lands above the Great Lakes were seen, rightly, as valuable for their lumber and minerals and, wrongly, as potential farmland. To lose what southerners were already calling "New Ontario" to Manitoba would be to strip the province of half its claimed territory and its guarantee of primacy within the Confederation. The Ontario government responded by recommending a border running due north from the American border, west of Lake of the Woods. Both sides agreed that some kind of arbitration was necessary; neither could agree on how to conduct it.

Knowing he would obtain far more favourable terms with a friendly Liberal than an unfriendly Conservative government in office in Ottawa, Mowat repeatedly pressured Mackenzie to agree to an arbitration panel that would settle the line. But Mackenzie dithered and was coming to the end of his first—and, as it turned out, final—mandate before he named his government's representative on the panel. By this time, Mowat's government had exhaustively researched the original grant to the Hudson's Bay Company, the terms of its acquisition by the crown, and the presence of the provincial and federal governments in the region, and concluded, remarkably, that the Ontario claim was just. Mowat himself argued the case before the arbitration panel, which unanimously concluded in Ontario's favour. But the rejoicing was short-lived. Both the federal Parliament and the Ontario legislature needed to affirm the new boundary, but before Mackenzie could do his duty, he was defeated in the general election of 1878. Macdonald, triumphantly returned as prime minister, soon made it clear he had no intention of implementing the agreed-upon line. Undaunted, the Ontario legislature passed a bill granting itself jurisdiction over the area and, over Ottawa's heated objection, began sending agents and inspectors to administer the lands. The scene was set for a confrontation that threatened to tear the newly minted Confederation apart.

More than just the boundary question irritated the Ottawa-Ontario relationship. Macdonald and Mowat also came to words over the use of the disallowance clause. Mowat later contended he had agreed during the Quebec Conference negotiations to give the federal government the power to disallow provincial legislation only because that power, as exercised by the prime minister's imperial predecessors, was effectively moribund. "The general understanding was that the Federal Government should have precisely the same power of disallowing Acts of the Provincial Legislatures as the Imperial Government previously had," he maintained, "but that it was to be seldom used. Those who know that the Imperial Government seldom used this power of Disallowance in later years had no idea that it would be so greatly abused by the Canadian Government as it has been."[18] The widespread use of the disallowance power by the federal government amounted to nothing more than an abuse of precedent and practice as old as responsible government in British North America itself. It was, to Mowat's mind, never more grievously abused than in the case of the Rivers and Streams Act.

Boyd Caldwell, a local timber magnate in the Ottawa Valley and a good Liberal, owned the timber rights on the banks of the local Mississippi River and wanted to use the stream to float his logs down to Ottawa. But Peter MacLaren, who also owned timber rights and was a good Conservative, had built a dam and slide so he could float his own timber. He didn't want Caldwell using his slide, and successfully went to court to stop him. This decision offended Oliver Mowat. If it were upheld, anyone making an improvement on a stream could become its de facto owner. So the Ontario legislature passed the Rivers and Streams Act, making it illegal for someone who had improved a stream to ban its use to others, provided a reasonable toll was paid. This legislation annoyed Sir John A., who objected to the provincial government limiting the property rights of citizens, especially Conservatives. The federal government disallowed the legislation, on the grounds that it violated "private rights and natural justice."[19] The Ontario government responded forcefully. Crown land was clearly within provincial jurisdiction, insisted the acting attorney general, Adam Crooks, and the province was fully within its constitutional rights to pass the act. Disallowance, the province maintained, should be invoked only when a provincial government exceeded its constitutional authority, or when its actions jeopardized the entire federation. The Ontario government passed the legislation again. Macdonald disallowed it again. Ontario passed it a third time. Ottawa disallowed it a third time. The governments were at an impasse.

With the two first ministers irreconcilable, things went from difficult to impossible. The Ontario government asserted the right to regulate the insurance industry. Ottawa responded that this was an area of federal jurisdiction. The Ontario Parliament awarded itself the power to issue liquor licences; the federal government asserted it would decide who got to give them out. Even the vexed question of who could appoint QCs re-emerged, with the federal government, and the new Supreme Court of Canada, asserting that the crown resided solely in the federal Parliament and that, "as Her Majesty forms no part of the Provincial Legislature as she does of the Dominion Parliament, no Act of any such Local Legislature can ... impair or affect her prerogative right to appoint Queen's Council in Canada."[20]

But these disputes paled in comparison with the boundary issue. Macdonald was determined to see that Ontario received not one square foot of the new northern region. On March 21, 1881, the dominion government unilaterally extended the boundary of Manitoba eastward to include all the territory that the arbitration panel had awarded to Ontario. Its motives were clear: to constrain Confederation's most obstreperous province by expanding the size of its weakest and newest member—and one over which, not coincidentally, the federal government still retained control of crown lands—while asserting the federal government's right to shape the laws and powers of the provinces, Ontario especially, as it saw fit.

The skein of disputes between Mowat and Macdonald became increasingly personal. "Mowat is thoroughly hostile," Macdonald complained. "He is the mere jackal to Blake's lion and must be met in the same spirit."[21] In an extreme moment the prime minister publicly dubbed the premier of Ontario "the little tyrant." Macdonald's loyal lieutenant in the provincial legislature, Conservative leader W.R. Meredith, described the Liberal premier's actions as "provocative of civil war." In response, Mowat warned that if the federal government continued to resist Ontario's manifest destiny of northwest expansion and self-government, Ontario would leave the Confederation. On January 26, 1882, he rose in the Ontario legislature and laid out his position:

> Confederation was well worth maintaining if the Constitution was faithfully administered, and if the Dominion Government would deal fairly and justly with [the provinces]. But if their power of passing laws within their own legitimate sphere was to be subject to the whim of a Minister or Ministers at Ottawa, and if they could not demand the large amount of property to which they were entitled without foregoing the advantages of Confederation, then it was not worth maintaining.[22]

For a moment, some feared it truly would come to civil war. Having called, fought, and won a provincial election in February 1883 on the issue of provincial rights and the northwest boundary, Mowat had dispatched police, land commissioners, and other officials to show the flag in the disputed territory. The dominion government, through its Manitoba surrogates, sent in its own officials. During one particularly tense moment, dubbed the Battle of Rat Portage—the town was wisely renamed Kenora—Ontario and Manitoba officials spent most of the day arresting each other, "to the imminent danger of the peace and of loss of life."[23]

Fortunately, it never came to blows that day, and Ontario's cause was immeasurably bolstered later that year when Manitoba switched sides. Unlike their Ontario cousins, Manitoba's leaders had correctly concluded that the disputed territory would never grow wheat or much of anything else. Since the federal government controlled their natural resources, the land's lumber and mineral potential held little appeal. Besides, an increasingly large portion of the province's population had emigrated from Ontario and resented Ottawa's bullying of the mother province. The Manitoba government joined Ontario in appealing the boundary question to the Judicial Committee of the Privy Council. In these early years of Confederation, England continued to be the locale of last resort for legal appeals. In fact, all the major disputes—the power of the lieutenant-governor, the issue of the liquor licences, the Rivers and Streams Act—finally made their way to the Privy Council. And it was on this legal field of battle that Ontario finally triumphed over and greatly diminished the federal government.

As attorney general as well as premier of Ontario, and as one of the best legal minds in the dominion, Mowat argued the most important cases before the Privy Council himself. The question, in essence, was how the British North America Act should be interpreted. On its face, Mowat acknowledged, the act gave the federal government all the powers it had been exercising to disallow provincial legislation and impose its will. But the BNA Act was itself the product of history, convention, and implicit assumptions. The provinces that joined together in Confederation had been self-governing societies under the British crown for decades previously. The very act establishing Upper Canada in 1791 envisioned an autonomous colony possessed of its own rights and liberties, Mowat maintained, and Ontario had enjoyed responsible government since 1841. In an effective reversal of the BNA clause reserving to the federal government all powers not specifically granted to the provinces, Mowat argued that the provinces themselves had granted to the federal government only those specific powers of which they had chosen to divest themselves at Confederation. The federal government, then, had no business attempting to interfere in the jurisdictions of the sovereign provinces of Canada. "I claim for the Provinces the largest power which they can be given," he argued. "It is the spirit of the B.N.A. Act and it is the spirit under which Confederation was agreed to. If there was one point which all parties agreed upon, it was that all local powers should be left to the Provinces and that all powers previously possessed by the Local

Legislatures should be continued unless expressly repealed by the B.N.A. Act."[24]

In each and every instance, the Judicial Committee decided in favour of Ontario over the federal government. In part, superior research and legal preparation on Ontario's part accounted for the victories. In the boundary dispute in particular, in which the Privy Council upheld the original arbitration award, the province had so outmanoeuvred the federal government in the framing of the question before the courts and the use of precedents that, in retrospect, the outcome was almost a foregone conclusion. But more than simple legal legerdemain was involved. The Privy Council, viewing the new dominion from the vantage point of the old imperial power, agreed that the original intent of Confederation was to unite its separate colonies in a compact, not to absorb them into a single union. Mowat's argument made sense to them, and they happily rewrote the original BNA Act through their decisions to reflect the reality as they and the provincial premiers had always seen it. Macdonald, convinced that the expunction of the provincial powers was only a matter of time, was blindsided by the old empire and by the government of the most powerful province in the Confederation. "What luck Mowat has had with the P.C.!" Macdonald lamented.[25] After the Privy Council decision awarding the Northwest to Ontario was announced in July 1884, the "little tyrant" paraded throughout the jubilant province. Welcoming arches erected by a well-organized Liberal Party were emblazoned with previous victories: "Escheats, Insurance, Licenses, Rivers and Streams."[26] And a triumphal ode was even composed to commemorate the victory: "The traitor's hand is at thy throat, Ontario, Ontario ..."[27]

Thereafter, the federal government gave up attempts to use its disallowance power against the provincial government. Eventually, as Blake and Mowat had hoped, the power withered away altogether from disuse. The compact theory of Confederation—a federation of provinces, each sovereign in its own areas of jurisdiction, which formed of their own free will a federal government, imbuing it with a separate and limited sovereignty—became the conventional wisdom. The precedents set in the clashes between Mowat and Macdonald were inherited by their successors. When, in 1909, enraged Ontario bankers and business leaders appealed to Wilfrid Laurier to disallow Premier James Whitney's legislation forcing public control of hydroelectric distribution in the province, the canny prime minister ruefully shook his head and declined. "The legislation is abominable," he agreed. But with the Rivers and Streams precedent in mind, Laurier reminded his critics that the federal government had no practical power to interfere in the internal affairs of a province acting within its jurisdiction. "My opinion still is that the power of disallowance should not be exercised, except in cases of extreme emergency," he stated, "and where the interests of the Dominion at large are likely to suffer. If the evil complained of is simply confined to private individuals, I think this should not be a reason for interference."[28]

By the eve of the First World War, Confederation had evolved into a creation beyond John A. Macdonald's worst nightmare. Powerful, independent provinces, sovereign within their own spheres, manipulated the rights of property, levied their own taxes—even income taxes, in a few cases—exploited their natural resources, and managed schools, hospitals, and relief for the poor, while a weak and ineffectual central government presided over not much of anything in the drab little capital on the banks of the Ottawa. Ontario, especially, had evolved into the aggressive, rapidly industrializing powerhouse that its citizens had always known it would be, stripping the north of lumber and nickel, and using the proceeds to fuel her industrial plant in the south. The future for the province looked as bright as the future for the federal government appeared dim.

Having served his province for twenty-four years as premier—a record that will not easily be broken—"the Grand Old Man" of Ontario politics agreed to join Laurier in 1896 in his successful campaign to win the national government for the Liberals. Mowat's political enemy, Sir John A., was dead, the province prosperous and at peace, and the veteran premier's political legacy secure. Mowat, at seventy-six, accepted elevation to the Senate and appointment as minister of justice. The greatest crisis facing the country and the new administration centred on the bitter controversy over protecting French-language education rights in Manitoba. Within three months, Laurier and Mowat had negotiated a compromise to the seemingly intractable dispute. His work done, Mowat semi-retired, permitting a grateful Laurier to appoint him lieutenant-governor of Ontario, where he served until his death in April 1903 at the age of eighty-two, ending as close to a perfectly successful political life as any statesman could wish.

Yet whatever else the feisty Ontario premier and the compliant British courts had stripped from the federal government, one power it unreservedly retained: national defence and the conduct of war. And war was what the twentieth century would be about. The coming carnage in Europe would be the best news the federalists had ever had. In the end, war and the aftermath of war would take away from the provinces—at least temporarily—much of what they had wrung from the federal government during the first decades of Confederation. War would turn the Ontario government from Ottawa's most dangerous political opponent to its staunchest ally, the heartland of a transformed and powerful Canadian federation.

But even that transformation would not last. Mowat's and Macdonald's heirs have wrestled over the tools of power to this very day. And, as the twentieth century gave way to the twenty-first, it would be Mowat's ghost that was smiling.

3

Ottawa Wins at War

On the quiet eve before the cataclysm of the First World War, Ontario could take a self-satisfied pride in its progress. The Confederation experiment, now that it had been recast to better reflect the province's position as its dominant and internally sovereign member, was turning out to be a splendid success. Although the Canadian economy was generally sluggish in the last three decades of the nineteenth century, Ontario's population continued to expand, from 1.6 million people at Confederation to 2.1 million by 1911. In 1910 most people who lived in Ontario had been born there. To a bedrock of Loyalist and British stock had been added a smattering of German and other continental Europeans. Thousands of French Quebecers had crossed the Ottawa River in search of better land; they had more success in taming the hills and marshlands of the lower Ottawa Valley than their Scottish predecessors had experienced and now numbered 10 per cent of the population. For the first time, the majority of the province's people lived in towns and cities. Ontario was already an urban, industrialized society.

The small factories that had cropped up across the province were consolidating into fewer and more powerful firms, employing about a quarter of the entire workforce. The most powerful firm of all was Massey-Ferguson, Canada's first great multinational company, based in Toronto and Brantford. Its dependable and affordable farm equipment broke the soil of the American as well as the Canadian prairie. But already an increasing number of manufacturers were Canadian subsidiaries of American firms, setting up shop in Ontario to jump over a 35 per cent wall on imports. A handful of Canadian automobiles—the Dickson, the Le Roy, the Russell, the Frontenac, the Iroquois—had been swamped by American imports such as Ford and General Motors, manufactured under licence in Windsor and Oshawa.

Before long, manufacturing began to take a back seat to the retail and service sector. By 1920, less than 30 per cent of Ontario's workers worked the land; about a quarter were in manufacturing, and more than 30 per cent were in trade and services. The great department stores Eaton's and Simpsons confronted each other across Toronto's Queen Street, while the Eaton's catalogue challenged the Bible as the most essential reading in rural homes. Although Toronto was still smaller than Montreal, where the big banks had their headquarters, Toronto already employed more workers than its rival in trade and finance.

Toronto, Ottawa, Hamilton, and London were clearly preeminent, but Ontario remained primarily a province of modest, prosperous towns and villages. While fortunes waxed and waned—an industry closed, a factory opened, a railroad brought new prosperity inland, a port town languished—the Ontario urban archetype could be found from Windsor to Pembroke, with only slight regional variation. Each was dominated by a main street of solid brick shops: dry goods stores, apothecaries, banks, a post office, town hall, and library. The roads were mostly unpaved, and fertilized by horses (only 23,700 motor vehicles were registered in Ontario in 1913). Off the main street, the inevitable three neighbourhoods radiated in precise Victorian grids. There was the fine part of town, with substantial brick homes boasting bay windows and gingerbread detailing set on pleasant streets shaded by stately oaks and maples, chestnuts and elms. Here lived local industrial magnates, the doctor, the banker, the lawyer, perhaps a particularly successful merchant. They dominated the social and political life of the town.

Then came a broad swath of respectable homes—most of them brick, some wood frame—on narrower but still ample lots, sufficient for the merchants, the ministers, the managers of the local firm. The factory worker, the barman, the policeman, the shop assistant, and the widow lived in small and simple white-painted houses on streets without sidewalks. Finally, there was always a shabby part of town, usually outside its urban fringe, where the outcasts lived in shacks, their children infrequent visitors to school, the policeman their constant bane. Apartment buildings and row housing were rare. Rich or poor, Ontario was a province of detached homes. The exception was the emerging slums, such as The Ward in downtown Toronto, where thousands of newly arrived Russian Jewish, southern Italian, Greek, and other immigrants crammed into unhealthy tenements and toiled in sweatshops. Priests and ministers, social workers and teachers all struggled to ease their misery and convert their children into "proper" Ontario citizens.

By the First World War, towns and cities across southern Ontario enjoyed electricity, sewers, and municipal water, with many homes boasting the priceless advantage of indoor toilets. Most farms continued to rely on kerosene, outhouses, and wells. There were tensions, less of class than of religion—the Protestant majority did not consort more than absolutely necessary with the Irish and Catholic minority—and life could be restrictive at times. But there were church suppers, summer fairs, and dances to occupy free days, and taverns, general stores, and livery stables for men in search of simpler entertainments. There were libraries for improving the mind, and visiting singers to entertain with classical and popular favourites in the opera and vaudeville houses. In the surrounding countryside, marginal land was already being abandoned and starting to return to bush.

With almost every arable acre of land under cultivation in southern Ontario, successive Ontario governments in the last half of the nineteenth century had attempted to colonize the Shield lands north of Lake Simcoe and west of the upper Ottawa River. Spurred on by wildly optimistic assessments of the initial surveyors, they pushed settlement roads into the Muskoka, Haliburton, and Renfrew districts, advertising extravagantly in British and American newspapers about free land for enterprising pioneers. But word of mouth travels fast, even over corduroy roads, and the first settlers to the districts quickly discovered they had inherited a harvest of stones and heartbreak. The rough lumbermen found more to interest them, however, penetrating each year deeper into the forests in search of the white and red pine prized by American and British markets. Lumber became a vital export in a province still heavily dependent on importing most of its goods.

The Canadian Pacific Railway also opened up the north to mineral exploration. Prospectors went into the bush in search of gold and silver, although what they found more often was iron, nickel, and copper. By the 1880s, mines surrounding Fort William were steadily shipping ore to the smelters in Sault Ste. Marie, while the nickel and copper deposits in Sudbury, first mined in the 1880s, were, by the turn of the century, worth $2 million a year. The northern towns were rough, their buildings and population transitory, their fortunes booming and busting with each new mineral strike or mine closure. Cobalt, 160 miles north of North Bay, boasted its own stock exchange in 1909, along with eleven hundred cases of typhoid fever, thanks to its primitive sanitation. The North remained only thinly populated and rootless, but its precious exports of lumber and minerals would help anchor the commercial fortunes of Toronto, eventually allowing it to challenge Montreal as the first city of the nation.

At Queen's Park, thirty-four years of unbroken Liberal rule had finally given way in 1905 to the Conservatives under James P.

Whitney, who would be remembered as the premier who unleashed the energy potential of both the Niagara Falls and the public crusader Adam Beck. Conservative or Liberal, Ontario's premiers fit a certain mould: a penchant for public works mitigated by a concern for a balanced budget. Progressive conservatism it would eventually be called.

The Judicial Committee of the Privy Council's rewriting of the terms of Confederation in Ontario's interest in 1884 had ensured sovereignty for the provinces in all fields they had not willingly transferred to the federal authority. With such an interpretation now accepted wisdom, the political centre of the province was firmly at Queen's Park. This provincial ascendancy was further confirmed as the visionary Beck began to mine the "white coal of Niagara"—the abundant energy potential of the great cataract, and of other potential hydroelectric sites on the Great Lakes, the St. Lawrence and Ottawa rivers, and the inland streams. Sir Wilfrid Laurier, though appalled by such massive intervention in Ontario's economic infrastructure by a state-owned enterprise, appeared to accede to Ontario's right to develop those resources—even those on national waterways, arguably a federal preserve—and to Ontario's effective nationalization of power.

In fact, Confederation was working well for Ontario at both the provincial and the national levels. George Brown, however much he might have risked the province's autonomy when he was swept up in the rush of events at Charlottetown and Quebec, was right in predicting that the national government would have to pay close attention to Ontario's interests. Although the opening up of the Prairies diluted Ontario's relative dominance within Confederation, the province, with 2.5 million souls, still represented 35 per cent of the national population. Ontario was one of the two essential partners in Confederation, Quebec being the other. Combined, they were the *sine qua non* of the federation, the couple without which nothing was possible. If the federal government ever acted in defiance of their interests, it would lose that fight. Ontario and Quebec, after all, held the ultimate sanction in any confrontation with the federal government or with the other provinces. They could leave—and they knew it. "There is no reason why Ontario should not be a nation if she were minded to be one," the historian and commentator Goldwin Smith had observed in 1891.[1]

An equally dangerous threat to the federation would have been conflict between Ontario and Quebec. It was their inability to get along that had led to the breakup of the first Canada and had launched Confederation. But, as in a marriage whose tensions ease once the spouses give each other more space and solitude, Ontario and Quebec had stopped bickering almost as soon as their forced union was severed, to be replaced by the looser ties of Confederation. Sir John A.'s attempts to consolidate federal power had, in part, been frustrated by the close cooperation between Mowat and the Quebec premier, Honoré Mercier. To Mercier we owe the invention of the conference of provincial premiers: a custom, now time honoured, in which the first ministers meet without the prime minister to complain about him and to approve a set of demands—a list that the prime minister then does his best to ignore. Back in 1887 Mercier had convened the first conference of premiers (British Columbia and Prince Edward Island stayed away) as he sought backing in his own campaign to force the federal government to revise its formula for provincial grants. Quebec was also struggling to protect its autonomy, but was heavily in debt and desperately in need of federal funds. Mercier's argument was compelling. In creating Confederation, the provinces had surrendered their power to collect customs and excise taxes, so as to give the federal government a source of income. The revenue now vastly exceeded the size of the federal grants back to the provinces. Mercier suggested that the provinces should join together at the conference to work out a new funding formula, which they would then demand the federal government implement, and to organize a system of common defence against "the centralizing tendencies manifested of late years by the Federal government."[2]

Mowat was wary of increasing federal transfers. His province was easily balancing its books with the revenues from timber licences, and any redistribution of transfer payments was bound to cost Ontario taxpayers money, since much of the federal government's revenues came from wealth generated by the province. But Mowat figured it would be worth the money to have Quebec and the other provinces onside in his own fight with the federal government over provincial powers, and he willingly attended the gathering in Quebec City. Although Macdonald studiously ignored the conference, an Ontario-Quebec axis had been forged, and the two provinces would come often to each other's defence. When Wilfrid Laurier threatened to disallow Ontario's moves to become the world's first jurisdiction to nationalize its electrical energy supply, future Quebec premier Louis-Alexandre Taschereau spoke passionately in Ontario's defence, prompting a grateful Whitney to promise: "You may depend on it that from that day forward the Provinces of Ontario and Quebec will be looked upon as standing together for the protection of everything relating to the Provinces."[3] Twenty years later, Taschereau and his Ontario counterpart, Howard Ferguson, would do similar and equally successful battle together to head off a federal attempt to regulate the insurance industry.

Provided the federal government kept its nose out of Ontario's business—and Ottawa's many losses in the courts, combined with the political cost of confronting the Ontario-Quebec axis, had made federal politicians wary of interfering in provincial affairs—Confederation had many benefits to offer Ontario. Since its members dominated the House of Commons in Ottawa, rivalled in numbers only by Quebec's, Confederation gave Ontario the chance it had never had before to influence policy in the Maritimes and to dominate the shape and pace of Western expansion. With each passing year, citizens in Atlantic Canada, and later in British Columbia and the Prairies, came increasingly to realize that they had become dependent on central Canada, and Ontario in particular. As the Maritimes' relative strength ebbed, and the West remained too fragile and underpopulated to assert its own destiny, that dependence only grew, to the benefit of imperial Ontario. By far the most emphatic expression of that imperialism was the National Policy.

In September 1873 a financial panic in New York had ushered in a five-year continental depression that flattened prices and slowed growth. The United States emerged from the depression before Canada. Although Ontario weathered the storm better than other parts of the new country, even there growth slowed to a near standstill. As a result, Ontarians made up their fair share of the one million Canadians who emigrated across the porous border to seek work in the United States. The Mowat government blamed Canada's lingering economic stagnation on the American tariffs on Canadian goods, and it urged the federal government to negotiate a reciprocity, or free trade, agreement with the United States. But the Americans weren't interested; the only proposal they were prepared to consider was a complete customs union, as an obvious first step to annexation. John A. Macdonald returned to power in 1878 by promising to take a very different tack. The government would push through a major transcontinental railway, linking the western territories and the newly arrived province of British Columbia to the Laurentian heartland, and would throw up high protective walls against the import of American or British manufactures. The tariffs would encourage the still-fragile manufacturing centres of southern Ontario and the Montreal area, and provide captive markets for their goods in the Maritimes and the West.

Ontario businessmen embraced the new policy with enthusiasm. Here was an alternative to the impenetrable American market, one uniquely favouring their own situation. Since Atlantic Canada was too remote and poor, Quebec's manufacturing base was steadily eroding in the face of competition from the more populous province next door, and western Canada was too sparsely populated to attract capital investment, Ontario manufacturers had little to fear from domestic competition. Tariffs would keep the only real threat, American manufacturers, out of the market.

The practical results of the National Policy are difficult to judge. In the short term, it may have had little effect at all. With a population of only 7.2 million in 1911, scattered across half a continent, Canada was too small and dispersed a market to sustain a major manufacturing economy. Indeed, the Canadian economy remained sluggish until the end of the nineteenth century, and the federal government might have done better to push harder for free trade. But whatever its tangible results, the National Policy quickly became entrenched as a national myth. The human and natural resources of the country flowed into the industrial heartland of Ontario—and, to a lesser extent, Montreal and its hinterlands—which fattened on the bounty. The western and eastern regions were further impoverished as their reluctant members were forced to buy overpriced goods with money borrowed from avaricious central Canadian bankers. Not only that, but they had to kow-tow to the swaggering politicians, businessman, and intellectuals of Toronto. The National Policy led everyone outside Ontario to identify it as "the eternal other—the cause of your problems, the imperial and imperious centre, the place where people live high off someone else's hog, the tilt in Confederation's pin-ball machine, the soulless place where your kids have to go to get work."[4]

This image suited Ontario just fine. Canada was a wonderful country, made more wonderful by the fact that the English-speaking parts of it were dominated by Ontario: by its politicians in Parliament, its banks, its publishing houses, magazines, and universities, its state of mind. As the century that Laurier said belonged to Canada began to unfold, Ontarians had every reason to feel quietly, comfortably happy with their place at the centre of things.

It could have gone on forever, but for the assassination of the Archduke Ferdinand in Sarajevo on June 28, 1914.

The one unambiguous, unshared, and undisputed right of the government of Canada is to wage war. It has never been suggested that provincial approval is required for the federal government to conduct diplomacy, including its ultimate means. When Britain declared war on Germany on August 4, 1914, Canada, which was still only a self-governing dominion within the empire, was automatically at war as well. Within weeks, Parliament had invoked the Emergency War Measures Act, suspending many of the civil liberties of the ancient and unwritten constitution, and the federal government proceeded to become the only game in town.

The nation was led by Robert Laird Borden, who was holidaying in Muskoka when news of the impending war forced him to rush back to the capital. Born of humble Nova Scotia stock, Borden had pushed himself to the top by exploiting his own keen intellect and rigid determination to succeed: educating himself in the classics and the law, rising to the top of a prominent Halifax law firm, entering Parliament out of a sense of duty and curiosity more than personal ambition, welding the shattered Conservative Party into an electable machine. A progressive, dedicated to nationalizing railways and modernizing the public service, Borden had not the slightest doubt about the right and duty of the federal government to wage war by all available means. On the two days before the declaration of war, Borden recalled that he and his cabinet "spent practically the whole day in Council. We established censorship, declared bank notes legal tender, authorized excess issue of dominion notes, empowered the proper officers to detain enemy ships, prohibited the export of articles necessary or useful for war purposes, and generally took upon ourselves responsibilities far exceeding our legal powers. All these measures, which were wholly without legal validity until they were afterwards ratified by Parliament, were accepted throughout the country."[5]

But it was war, of course. Provincial concerns were swept aside in the life-and-death struggle of the British Empire, France, and Russia to contain the Central Powers. Emigration to the Prairies had pushed Ontario's population down to 31 per cent of the total, yet the province sent more than 40 per cent of the troops who made up the 600,000-strong Canadian Army. Of those Ontario men in uniform, 68,000 died or were wounded, a frightening figure for a province unused to war. The trauma of that loss remains etched today in the names on stone plaques on the carefully tended war memorials found in every town and village across the province.

Passions ran high. Ontarians of German descent found that resorts wouldn't accept their reservations; German professors were barred from classes; and the city of Berlin changed its name to Kitchener. Under the War Measures Act, suspect "aliens" could be, and were, held without benefit of habeas corpus. Moreover, the war was far from universally popular. Farmers resented the loss of farmhands to work their fields, especially since the population of rural townships was already in decline. (Grey County, for example, had lost 50 per cent of its population between 1900 and 1910.) They took their revenge when the war ended by helping to elect Ontario's first and last farm-labour coalition.

But Ontario was not Borden's problem. His main concern was the French. Quebecers (and francophones in eastern Ontario) had little sympathy for a war that, for them, was simply another intrigue by imperial Britain. Fully anticipating the national crisis it would cause, Borden held off imposing conscription for as long as possible. But his stern, Christian, Conservative duty was to the troops, and it broke his heart when he visited thousands of wounded and dying Canadians in British hospitals. The maw of war was inexorable; 15,464 Canadians were lost during the failed Passchendaele campaign alone.

Borden was determined to support his armies overseas at whatever political cost. With the pool of volunteers exhausted, the government introduced conscription in 1917. It almost severed the country. Army troops with machine guns had to be called in to quell riots in Quebec, where four people were killed in demonstrations. Conscription destroyed the Conservative Party in Quebec and launched the province down its winding nationalist road. It had, however, the opposite effect in Ontario, which would never have forgiven Borden had he *not* supported the troops by bringing in conscription. Canada, at least in the eyes of its English citizens, grew up during the First World War. Canadian troops were at first thrown into the British ranks, and the Canadian government learned about the progress of the war by reading the newspapers, but Borden pressed steadily for a more independent role. Canadian troops fought under their own commanders at Vimy Ridge, captured from the Germans in April 1917 after both the British and the French had failed. By the end of the war Canada, along with the other dominions, sat on the Imperial War Cabinet, and the Canadian Parliament independently ratified the Treaty of Versailles. Canada had come of age.

Borden was no less determined to pursue all means necessary to finance the war, which, at its peak, was costing the federal government $1 million a day. Grants to the provinces were sharply curtailed, and Ottawa gave itself a virtual monopoly in the bond market. But the most drastic measure by far, and the one with the greatest long-term impact, was Borden's decision in 1917 to impose a national income tax.

While the British North America Act gave the provinces explicit power to tax incomes—and by the outbreak of war a few had already imposed such taxes—it granted the federal government the power to raise revenue by any means it chose. To force men to fight on foreign soil, without taxing the income of those safely at home, seemed obscene. In 1917 the Borden government imposed a national tax on incomes, promising taxpayers and provincial premiers that the new levy was only temporary, an emergency measure to tide the government through the war. Little more than a year later, however, the federal government decided that the tax would be permanent. Canada's debt stood at an appalling $2.5 billion. The tax would not only have to be entrenched but sharply increased. There would be no larger subsidies to the provinces, although Ottawa did grant the western provinces control over their natural resources while retaining the subsidy it had been paying in lieu. (All this was galling to Ontario, since its taxpayers funded much of the transfer, just as they had the earlier subsidies to the Maritimes.) When Borden reluctantly agreed in 1919 to increase payments to the provinces, he stipulated that the money must go to highways and housing for the 600,000 returning veterans. In this way the notorious federal conditional grants were born: federal funding in areas of provincial jurisdiction tied to federal rules and conditions. There is only so much tax room (the capacity for individuals and businesses to pay taxes). By absconding with the income tax, and then transferring the revenues back to the provinces in the form of conditional grants, Ottawa had vastly increased its influence over the provincial governments. The Ontario government, faced with the task of finding jobs and housing for its returning soldiers, had no choice but to accept the money and plead for more.

Queen's Park had not, however, been utterly quiescent during the war. Labour shortages extended beyond the farm, and workers were scarce everywhere. Children were excused from classes to work in the fields, and women took over many of the jobs usually reserved for men—their first great infusion into the workforce. Banks quickly found that women made particularly good tellers, but they also earned their pay in the munitions factories. The mobilization of women into the workforce bolstered the demands of the suffragette movement, which increased pressure on Premier William Hearst until the amiable and politically ineffectual premier abruptly reversed himself in 1917 and granted women the vote. Ottawa followed soon after. Hearst also succumbed to the strange coalition of suffragettes, Christian farmers, and social activists who demanded an end to the ills of alcohol, imposing prohibition in 1916. The only exemption was for medicinal purposes, prompting a mysterious increase in sales at pharmacies. By the time the Americans launched their prohibition experiment in 1920, pressure was already mounting inside a thirsty Ontario for a relaxation of the ban.

Ontario and the other provinces had surrendered much during the Great War, and would never fully succeed in recapturing the fiscal sovereignty they had ceded to Ottawa during those years. But with the return of peacetime, Ontario premiers regained their determination to be masters in their own house. Men were back at their jobs, women were back in the home—although now they could be seen smoking in public—the twenties were roaring, and demand was high for new roads to accommodate the Model Ts, schools to accommodate the sudden boom in babies, and hospitals to accommodate the sick, who were living longer thanks to rapid advances in surgery and public health. Cities were growing: workers commuted to downtown Toronto from as far away as Eglinton Avenue and beyond. Vaudeville theatres gave way to movie houses, and even in rural areas electricity was increasingly the norm. Factories sprouted to supply the burgeoning demand for newfangled washing machines, refrigerators, and vacuum cleaners.

For most of the decade, Ontario was governed by one of its most successful premiers, Howard Ferguson, a large, hearty man from Kemptville in the Ottawa Valley, whose jovial disposition masked a sharp political cunning. He brought his Conservatives to power in 1923, following a bold but drastically unsuccessful attempt by labour and farmers to govern through the short-lived protest party known as the United Farmers of Ontario. A government that was suspicious of roads (they took boys off the farm) and had to borrow its attorney general from another party, since lawyers were banned in its own, could not be long for this world. After four contentious years under Premier Bud Drury, the UFA disappeared into trivia.

Ferguson, however, was a far more substantial leader. A cautious moderate, he gradually dismantled prohibition, promising a parched but wary population that his government would keep tight control over the sale and distribution of alcohol. Provincially owned liquor stores offered a limited and heavily taxed selection of approved beer, wines, and spirits, while restaurants remained dry (at least officially) and only men were allowed to drink in seedy, dimly lit beer rooms.

Ferguson, like most provincial premiers of the time, was far more aggressive in the area of public spending. While the cautious new Liberal prime minister, William Lyon Mackenzie King, actually reduced federal spending by 5 per cent, total provincial revenues soared by 105 per cent. Ferguson's government not only paved roads, increased teachers' salaries, and built new hospitals, but it expanded the three public universities (University of Toronto, Queen's University, and University of Western Ontario) and levied a broad new range of amusement, or "sin," taxes, along with the first provincial income tax.

Ferguson's greatest ambition was to extend hydroelectric power in Ontario. With the Niagara gorge fully exploited, the next goal was to harness the power of the St. Lawrence and Ottawa rivers. But would Ottawa consent? And how would Quebec respond? Ferguson took the traditional approach of a compact federalist: he cut a deal with Quebec, tempering regulations that limited the teaching of French in French-language schools in exchange for Premier Taschereau's support on the power issue. Ultimately, Ontario agreed to import its energy from Quebec, while at a dominion-provincial conference in 1927 King acknowledged the rights of Ontario and Quebec to develop power on the St. Lawrence. King, in exchange, wanted finally to bring the Canadian Constitution home from Westminster. Not only did he fail, but his successor,

R.B. Bennett, went so far in 1932 as to acknowledge that the constitution could not be amended without provincial consent—a triumph for the compact-theory school.

But, by then, provincial power would once again be in a long, slow decline, precipitated by a new war—this one not military, but economic.

The worldwide industrial decline that came to be known as the Great Depression hurt the United States, Germany, and Canada more than any other country. In Canada, as in the United States, the economic price of over-expansion of industry, protective tariffs, and a weak banking system was further complicated by severe drought in the western provinces. The national income declined by almost half between 1929 and 1931. Everywhere, times were hard.

As property taxes dried up, municipalities were forced to default on bond payments. The Ontario government, although not as desperate as its bankrupt western counterparts, struggled to stay afloat while providing relief for the unemployed. The federal government doled out reluctant help, as it repeatedly reminded the provinces that poor relief was a matter entirely within their jurisdiction. To absorb the glut of surplus workers, Ontario punched a railway north towards James Bay, built airports for northern towns, and pushed Highway 17 across the rocky Shield. Thousands of unemployed men flocked unwillingly to work camps in the northern bush, which became incubators of militant unionism and the new Communist Party of Canada. Many of those still employed, especially in the middle class of Orange Ontario, blamed the workers for their own misfortune.

Everywhere, the politicians ill-fitted the times. George Stewart Henry, the Conservative successor to Howard Ferguson, was a successful dairy farmer, but from the same pinstriped cloth as American president Herbert Hoover and Canadian prime minister R.B.

Bennett. The Depression baffled him as much as it did other conservative politicians across the continent. It didn't help when Henry was forced to reveal that he owned $25,000 in the stock of a company that placed him in a conflict of interest. He'd simply forgotten he owned the stock, he told the House in deep embarrassment. It was impolitic in a depression to confess one could lose track of $25,000.

Henry told a first ministers' conference in 1933 that his province's revenues had declined by $6 million since 1929, his government would be forced to suspend public works programs, and the federal government should come to the aid of the provinces. Bennett, imitating Hoover, refused. Two years later, however, in an attempt to mimic the charismatic new American president, Franklin Delano Roosevelt, Bennett announced his own New Deal–style national program of unemployment and social insurance, a national minimum wage, and a limit to the hours of work. The courts duly struck the whole thing down, just as the American courts struck down much of Roosevelt's New Deal, but by then Bennett was but a bad memory. Mackenzie King, staging a remarkable political comeback, had returned his Liberal Party to power to confront the economic and increasingly constitutional crises that afflicted the troubled dominion.

Back in 1932, King, as Liberal opposition leader, had invited Mitchell Hepburn, a former MP and now the young Liberal opposition leader in Ontario, to dinner at Laurier House, suggesting that he bring along Mrs. Hepburn and a few friends. Hepburn, a farm boy from Elgin County with little education and few manners, showed up with a bunch of pals, far more than the fastidious King could seat at his dinner table. King diplomatically shrugged off the embarrassment, but it was a sign of things to come. "From the beginning, Mitch Hepburn, an undisciplined young man with a quick intelligence complicated by emotions bordering on the juvenile, could never hope to understand the cautious, calculating King," wrote Hepburn's first biographer. "... For his part, Mackenzie, ever readier to boast of friendship than to experience it, never comprehended or fully trusted the bumptious member from Elgin."[6]

Over the course of the next ten years, the relationship between Hepburn and King deteriorated from alliance to antagonism to deep and bitter enmity. It was not King's fault. Canada's longest-serving and arguably most successful prime minister survived three decades of political life by avoiding, at almost any cost, making enemies. King may have had his eccentricities—including a fondness for ruins, seances, and perhaps ladies of the evening—but he guided Canada through the Roaring Twenties, the back half of the Depression, and the Second World War by exercising the arts of compromise he had perfected as a young labour negotiator. He practised moderation in all things, even in conversations with the dead, seeking always to navigate a way forward while avoiding political shoals. He tried to work with Hepburn, as he tried to work with all his rivals. In the end, he simply couldn't understand him. But who could?

Mitch Hepburn possessed much of what King lacked. While the prime minister fretted over his inability to rouse the population through the force of his words, Hepburn's oratory could breathe fire, and he never lost the love and the loyalty of what he called "the little people on the back concessions." While King mourned the solitude of his life and the absence of real friends, Hepburn revelled in hanging out with the boys from Yarmouth Township, as well as the girls who frequented the King Edward Hotel, where he lived as premier. But what King possessed most, a Christian commitment to virtue and an inner sense of balance, Hepburn lacked utterly. Sensitive, cruel, erratic, charming, politically shrewd, ultimately paranoid—the Huey Long of Canadian politics, the newspapers called him—Mitch Hepburn was the most eccentric premier in Ontario history. "Mitch was a sinner," acknowledged one former supporter, "but he wasn't what you'd call a bad man."[7]

Gifted with the populist touch that King could never master, Hepburn retained the loyalty of the voters through a premiership of eight years of profound confusion. The people loved him because he sold off the ministerial limousines and the mansion of the lieutenant-governor. He also provided a home for the Dionne Quintuplets, the miracle babies of a poor French Canadian family from Corbeil, in Northern Ontario, who diverted a glum nation from the dreary realities of difficult times. The people accepted his well-meaning failures, repeated reversals, and generally ineffectual government. (His only real accomplishments were to balance the province's books and introduce pasteurization of milk.) And Ontarians seemed positively forgiving as, with each passing year, he spent less time on his duties as premier and more hanging out with the boys (and girls). Almost certainly, his mind deteriorated towards the end, brought on in part by drink. Even at his peak, he was unpredictable and at times dangerous. Although a populist, he became a staunch enemy of unions and harboured paranoid fears of communist conspiracies. Not surprisingly, throughout his tenure, relations with Ottawa were in a constant uproar. Hepburn's initial obsequious support for King quickly turned into dark suspicion and delusional obsession, until finally his actions could only be characterized as "the product of an imagination diseased and warped by hatred for King."[8]

They fought over everything, but mostly over power—literal and political. For years, Toronto had bickered with Ottawa over who had the right to develop the enormous energy potential of the Great Lakes–St. Lawrence waterways. To Ottawa, they were navigable bodies of water and international boundaries, a clear federal preserve, while to Queen's Park they were natural resources, within the provincial domain. Howard Ferguson had bought temporary peace by agreeing to purchase electricity from Quebec. But then the Depression hit, and it appeared that Ontario had purchased and was paying for electricity it didn't need. To make matters worse, there may have been some shady dealings in the signing of the contracts. Hepburn rose to victory in the 1934 election promising to clean up the mess at Queen's Park. Shortly after taking office, his government introduced legislation repudiating the Quebec contracts.

This was not a wise move. Not only did it erode investor confidence in Ontario's finances and make the government vulnerable to lawsuits, but, even as the legislature debated the bill, Hepburn was receiving warnings from his officials that, as Ontario industry slowly staggered to its feet in the last years of the Great Depression, energy use was increasing again. Without the Quebec supply, the province would soon face a serious energy shortage. The pig-headed premier forced through the legislation anyway, but, as the shortage grew imminent and the courts struck down Hepburn's attempts to legislate against legal challenges to his actions, the government was forced to retreat. Ultimately, it renegotiated much the same deal that the legislation had struck down, although on slightly better terms. Meanwhile, the experts at Hydro had hit on their own scheme to solve the emerging energy crisis: Ontario would divert streams flowing into Hudson Bay and send the water into the Great Lakes instead, thereby increasing waterflow and providing more power at the Niagara station.

Such a massive diversion required American consent, which King actually tried to get for Hepburn. The Ontario Liberal premier, after all, had been a young and devoted MP in King's caucus in the 1920s, and the politically sensitive prime minister was anxious to keep relations between the federal and the Ontario wings of the Liberal Party cordial. The Americans, however, were only interested in discussing a new, deepwater seaway for the Great Lakes, a plan that required the approval of Ontario and Quebec as well as the two national governments. Hepburn, who rarely met a good idea that he liked, vetoed the proposal, calling it extravagant. But then the energy experts realized that the watershed diversion, coupled with the new contracts with Quebec, would soon give Ontario an energy surplus again. To stave off what was quickly turning into a major demonstration of his and his government's incompetence, Hepburn hit on the notion of selling the extra energy to the United States. But Ontario had a long-standing policy of resisting energy exports, since it would, in the long term, be disadvantageous to share its energy with its American competitors. The sale would require an energy agreement between Canada and the United States, and the approval of the federal government. Hepburn travelled to Ottawa to pitch the proposal to his fellow Liberals in cabinet, and King went to Hepburn's hotel room personally to tell him that the cabinet had turned him down. Hepburn had already been deeply, though unjustifiably, wounded when King rejected his suggestion that one of his friends be appointed to the federal cabinet. This further rejection was proof that King, once his idol and mentor, was now his enemy.

The hydro mess solved itself. With the outbreak of war in 1939, the Canadian, American, and Ontario governments agreed to expand the province's hydroelectric potential at Niagara and elsewhere. But the federal government's treatment of the issue inflamed Hepburn's animus towards King. When the Rowell-Sirois Commission was appointed to look into constitutional renewal, that ill-will deepened into the darkest well of discord ever to afflict Ontario-federal relations.

The need for some fundamental changes to the Canadian Constitution had been apparent since the end of the First World War. It was clear to any impartial observer that a dangerous imbalance had entered into the responsibilities and resources of the two levels of government. The economic downturn that followed the First World War, the expansion of provincial spending during the 1920s, and the virtual collapse of the economy that followed with the Depression had left the provincial governments struggling to provide relief for the poor, the unemployed, and the indigent elderly. The Fathers of Confederation, when they assigned the provincial governments responsible for schools, hospitals, and "charities," never imagined they were bestowing on them principal responsibility for creating the twentieth-century welfare state. With the federal government dominating the taxation field, the provinces were left with only a minority share of the income tax, plus gasoline and liquor taxes and licence fees to pay for their needs. They had no choice but to cut back on public works and poor relief. The federal government reluctantly sent grants to the provinces to help them with their efforts, while chafing at being unable to direct or take credit for the use of the funds. To Ottawa and many of the poorer provinces, the answer was simple: the federal government should take over responsibility for unemployment, poor relief, and public works. Successive Ontario and Quebec premiers had demanded the opposite: Ottawa should surrender its taxing authority and let them get on with the job. It was an argument as old as Mowat and Macdonald.

With each passing year of economic depression, the paralysis of government became more obvious and intolerable. Successive federal-provincial conferences had achieved nothing. Most people agreed that the country needed a national program of unemployment insurance, and even Hepburn conceded that Ottawa should have responsibility for the program. But Mackenzie King wanted more. A permanent reallocation of roles and responsibilities was in order, the re-elected prime minister concluded after yet another dominion-provincial conference ended in failure. In 1937 he launched the Royal Commission on Dominion-Provincial Relations, to be headed by Newton Rowell, chief justice of Ontario. (When Rowell became ill, he was succeeded by Joseph Sirois, a law professor at Laval University.) The commission began its work just as relations between Hepburn and King began to crumble—over the power issue and Hepburn's belief that Ottawa hadn't provided him with enough support when he sought to suppress a strike at General Motors in Oshawa. Hepburn was convinced that the strike, part of the rising union movement in the province, was a threat to peace, order, and good government. The federal government sent Hepburn RCMP reinforcements to aid the local police, but baulked when Hepburn demanded even more federal muscle. Infuriated, Hepburn expelled the RCMP and recruited his own squad of special constables from among the ranks of war veterans and university students. Thankfully "Hepburn's Hussars" (also known as "the Sons of Mitch") were never required. General Motors and the United Auto Workers negotiated a settlement. Big Labour had come to Ontario, but the situation deepened Hepburn's resentment of King.

When the Rowell-Sirois Commission visited Toronto in May 1938, Hepburn was waiting. He had already had numerous conversations with Duplessis, the equally colourful and ambitious premier of Quebec, and the two agreed that the commission was nothing more than the latest attempt by Ottawa to undermine the rights and privileges of the Two Provinces That Mattered in Confederation, to steal their revenues to rescue the bankrupt provinces in the Maritimes and the West.

There have been few affronts to the dignity of the federal power and the rights of the smaller provinces to match the performance before the commission that day at Queen's Park. Hepburn swaggered into the committee room, bellicose and belligerent. First he questioned the validity of the commission's existence, insisting that dominion-provincial conferences were the best means of reforming a constitution, if it must be reformed. Then he went on to argue against any further centralizing of powers at the federal level. "For we are a stupid people if we imagine ourselves immune from the consequences of concentrating power in a few hands. The accumulation of power leads to autocracy; its distribution is the safety-zone of democracy." Social services were the responsibility of the provincial government, he reminded the commissioners, and the federal government could serve best by returning its income-taxing power to the provinces. "The provinces charged with social services should make the initial levy on incomes arising within the provinces," he argued. "The federal income-taxing officer should step in only when the provincial needs have been satisfied." Finally, the attempts to equalize social services across the country were ill-advised, since "equality between provinces is impossible." If other provinces lacked the resources to manage their economies without federal help, "the remedy that first suggests itself is amalgamation."[9]

Then he threw them all a party, and got drunk.

This was nothing compared with Hepburn's performance when the Rowell-Sirois report was finally tabled in 1940. (The Rowell-Sirois Commission established an early and enduring precedent for royal commissions taking much longer to complete their mandate than anyone expected or reason suggested.) By then, much turbulent water had passed under the dominion-provincial bridge. Canada once again was at war against Germany, and relations between King and Hepburn were so poisonous they had prompted a general election. On Thursday, January 8, 1940, Hepburn shocked most of his own back bench by rising in the legislature and demanding that it pass a motion censuring the federal government for failing to prosecute the war with sufficient vigour. Many Liberal MPPs hid out in the lobby rather than voting to condemn a fellow Liberal government and the chief executive of a nation fighting for its life. Several even voted against the leader. But the resolution carried with the help of George Drew's Conservatives—Drew hated federal Liberals even more than provincial ones—and King, who had been looking for an excuse to call an election, immediately dissolved Parliament, claiming he needed a fresh mandate as war leader. The Liberals won an overwhelming victory, particularly in Ontario. It was a quietly triumphant King who met Hepburn and the provincial premiers in the chamber of the House of Commons on January 14, 1941, for a dominion-provincial conference to discuss the implications of the long-awaited report of the commission.

Although Hepburn, and perhaps even King, had not fully realized it, the Canada and the Ontario that went to war in 1939 were markedly different from the emerging dominion that took up arms in 1914. The federal Parliament, in a gesture of independence, had waited one full week after Great Britain had gone to war with Hitler's Germany before declaring that it, too, was at war with the Third Reich. The delay reflected the growing maturity of the nation. In Ontario, its industrial heart, there were now 4,000 miles of paved roads and more than 704,000 automobiles. There were steel plants in Hamilton and Sault Ste. Marie, and auto plants in Oshawa, Oakville, and Windsor. The province was thoroughly urban: 60 per cent of its population lived in cities of over 30,000 people. And 90 per cent of urban homes had indoor toilets, whereas 87 per cent of farms still relied on outdoor privies—a further impetus to migration. By 1941, with France defeated and the United States and Soviet Union still neutral, Canada was the Allies' second-largest supplier of men and material.

As war demand strained the limits of the nation's resources, new investment focused on expanding industry. The federal government poured billions of dollars into Ontario. Steel and auto plants grew enormously, iron ore and nickel mines were at full production. The government compensated for a shortage of rubber caused by the Japanese conquest of the East Indies by establishing a massive petrochemical works at Sarnia. The National Steel Car Company near the Toronto airport at Malton became a major centre for airplane production, specializing in the Lancaster bomber. The energy surplus changed to an energy shortage, with electricity rationing keeping houses cool and gas rationing emptying the new Queen Elizabeth Way, Canada's first four-lane highway, from Toronto to Niagara Falls. Everything was rationed: cuffs on pants were banned; short skirts became fashionable, to the joy of men still around to appreciate them; sugar was at a premium; and the lack of material for civilian clothing even produced a severe shortage of children's underwear.

If the war had greatly expanded the federal budget and the federal debt, many provinces remained financially precarious. New Brunswick was in real danger of defaulting on its debt, and the precedent could well lead to a string of provincial defaults and a crisis of confidence in the nation's finances. The Rowell-Sirois recommendation was simple: the provinces should surrender virtually all taxing authority, along with responsibility for employment and social services. The federal government, in exchange, would assume all provincial debt and provide equalization grants to poorer provinces to ensure national standards in areas under provincial jurisdiction. For any Ontario premier, such a surrender of provincial autonomy would be inconceivable; for Hepburn, it was an act of war. Even he accepted that, during the war, the federal government would need additional authority to tax, but that was no excuse for permanently handing over the keys to the treasury. Hepburn came to the 1941 dominion-provincial conference not to attend it, but to wreck it. No sooner had King finished his innocuous opening remarks than Hepburn rose to denounce the commission, the conference, and King in terms considered offensive even for him.

To be discussing amendments to the Canadian Constitution while the Allied forces were wrestling with mortal foes was obscene, Hepburn contended. "Is this the time to send a courier to bomb-torn London with a document in his hand and have him step in the Hall of Westminster and ask the British Parliament to pause in its consideration of questions determining the very life of the British Empire in order to debate the question of a new Constitution for Canada?" He condemned the report's recommendations as an act of "national vandalism" and, playing on the Ontario-Quebec axis, warned that the report would damage Quebec's ability to defend its culture. He promised that Ontario would "stand solidly beside Quebec if at any time her minority rights were threatened."

Shortly thereafter, the Ontario delegation announced it was walking out of the conference. With a fine rhetorical flourish,

Hepburn concluded: "There is no alternative open to my colleagues and myself but to withdraw and leave these wreckers of Confederation under the guise of patriotism to continue to carry on their nefarious work."[10]

King quietly declared that, under the circumstances, there was no reason to continue the conference. But the prime minister was far from unhappy. He had publicly attempted to reach a compromise with the provincial governments, and they had walked—no, stormed—away. With the country at war, there was no more time for negotiations. The federal budget brought down in April 1941 announced the government's intention to initiate a Wartime Tax Agreement. The provinces were required to surrender all authority over personal and income taxes; in exchange, the federal government would provide grants to help them meet their obligations. Hepburn, by now deeply unpopular with the public and other politicians, had no choice but to agree or be branded a traitor. Ontario signed the agreement, after months of acrimonious negotiations. By the end of the war Ontario had joined the other provinces in agreeing that Ottawa should also take over sole and permanent control of unemployment insurance. The federal government now had all the powers Mackenzie King could dream of.

But Hepburn, however boorish and erratic he might have been, had at least preserved the principle of provincial sovereignty. Throughout his many bitter fights with King, he had stoutly defended Ontario's right to manage its own responsibilities and had successfully resisted federal efforts to force the provinces to permanently surrender their jurisdictions. In this he was simply defending—somewhat flamboyantly—Ontario's rights as others had before him. There was nothing, apart from the venom, of which Mowat or Whitney or Ferguson would have disapproved.

Still, the tide was running against Ontario. Modern times were centralizing times. War, economic depression, technology, fashion—they all favoured the head-office tendency, the experts at the top who could manage society like a well-run machine, if only they had the levers at their disposal. It was a philosophy that was anathema to Ontario's best interests, yet one the province would increasingly be unable to resist. Ultimately, its citizens would even come to embrace it.

4

"Does Ontario Exist?"

Leslie Frost, treasurer in the Conservative government that finally put an end to Hepburn Liberalism, sat at the right hand of Premier George Drew as yet another dominion-provincial conference came to its dispiriting end, silently disagreeing with his boss.

Mackenzie King, seventy and weakening in body if not in spirit, had been determined to make one last effort to expand the federal spending power and its control over social programs. With victory in Europe complete, and in the Pacific assured, King called a meeting of first ministers on August 6, 1945, to discuss how Canada should be governed after the war. Federal expectations were high, for the Second World War had transformed Canada. At grievous cost—the names of 42,042 war dead were added to the plaques on the war memorials—the country had progressed from a semi-dependent dominion gripped by chronic economic depression to a major sovereign state, the host of Allied conferences, one of the three major powers to land armies at Normandy. Canada at the end of the war had the world's fourth largest navy. Canadian diplomats participated actively in the framing of the United Nations charter. And, to their great good fortune, Canada and the United States were the two largest countries whose industrial infrastructure had not been devastated by bombing or invasion or both.

It was also the era to centralize. A country mired in a prolonged financial slump had been transformed by the mobilization for total war. The federal government had raised a mighty army, navy, and airforce and had ruled over a militarized economy that equipped and sustained a great war machine. There was a new mood in the air, a new spirit of optimism and confidence that experts in suits, within both the private sector and the federal public service, would guide Canada through the postwar challenges of accommodating the troops returning home from overseas, sustaining industry to prevent a postwar slump, and exploiting the power of the new knowledge—synthetics, antibiotics, nuclear energy—generated by the war. Canada needed roads, airports, power, and the endlessly debated but never built St. Lawrence waterway. It did not, in the minds of many, need ill-tempered obstruction from governments that were provincial in every sense of the word.

With the recommendations of the Rowell-Sirois Commission available as precedent and guide, and the war economy as proof of capability, the federal government hoped to retain all the enormous new powers it had accumulated over the previous five years. A federal green paper produced by the confident young men who now surrounded and dominated King proposed that Ottawa should become the only government with major taxing authority, responsible for employment, social policy, and economic development as well as its traditional roles of defence, customs, foreign relations, and regulation of the money supply. The proposal was breathtakingly audacious. The problem was George Drew.

"Colonel" George Drew, a man of imperial height and military bearing, always happiest wearing a red-and-blue military tie, of Loyalist stock and Guelph origin, was in many ways a progressive. He scrawled his "twenty-two points," legend has it, on the back of an envelope during the 1943 campaign, when the new Co-operative Commonwealth Federation, precursor to the New Democratic Party, appeared set to defeat both the old-line parties. Drew's response was a broad-based platform of municipal reform, improved access to education, broadened public health, subsidized housing, increased pensions, strengthened labour rights, agricultural marketing boards, and tax incentives for northern mining and lumbering—a program that successive Progressive Conservative governments would spend the next forty-two years implementing and expanding, making the party one of the most entrenched in any democratic nation. All Drew needed to implement his plan was for the federal government to relinquish its taxing powers and abandon its pretension to manage social policy.

If Drew was progressive socially, he remained "the last uncompromising defender of the Ontario region state."[1] Worse, he hated King almost as much as Hepburn had. Drew once wrote of King, "The more I see of him the more I wonder no one has yet been tried for some major criminal offence in carrying out their natural instincts in his presence."[2] And Drew, who harboured a deep suspicion of Quebec and its people, also suspected that King was planning to placate French Canada—the Second World War conscription crisis had come almost as close to wrecking the country as had that of the First—by bribing it with money siphoned from Ontario taxpayers.

Not only was Drew incensed at the proposals contained in the green paper—which also suggested making Ottawa responsible for pensions, social security, and major public works—but his worst suspicions were confirmed as he watched cabinet ministers conspiring in whispered asides with the aides in the chairs behind them. The new federal bureaucracy—the experts and the technocrats—were the real power behind the aging government. Drew would have none of it. In response, he not only demanded that the provinces retain their traditional powers and responsibilities but proposed a National Adjustment Fund, through which "have" provinces would transfer needed money to "have-not" provinces by means of a council of provincial ministers. Ottawa would actually have no role in what was becoming its favourite pastime—devising and implementing equalization programs.

The boys in suits were stunned. Drew was clearly attempting to revive the compact theory of Confederation—surely by now, they thought, an outmoded concept. And his National Adjustment Fund would act as "an open blank cheque on the Dominion treasury," one of them fumed, "to be signed not by the Dominion Parliament, but by a committee with nine Provincial Premiers on it, or worse still, nine provincial Legislatures."[3]

Ontario was not alone in its assault on the federal proposals. Drew found his anti-Quebec bias transformed as Maurice Duplessis joined him in defending the sovereignty of the provinces. Suddenly Drew was describing the Quebec strongman as "one of the most attractive companions one could ever meet."[4] The old Ontario-Quebec axis was alive and well, guaranteeing that the conference would end, once again, without agreement.

While Leslie Frost also objected to the terms the federal government was offering, he was more of a pragmatist than his stiff-necked premier. Possession is nine-tenths of political power, and the federal government, thanks to the necessities of war, now effectively possessed the sole power to tax income. It was clear that Mackenzie King had no intention of handing it back. Under the circumstances, as the treasurer quietly advised the premier, Ontario might do well to accept reality and negotiate terms. If the federal government agreed to take over unemployment insurance and to fund a national old age pension, both popular ideas to voters, then perhaps Ontario could surrender its powers of direct taxation. "Now is the time to negotiate," he urged Drew after the latest federal proposal—fundamentally similar to the earlier one—arrived in 1946. "... Our people are war weary. They have had 10 years of turmoil. They want what [British politician] Bonar Law referred to as *Tranquility*."[5] But tranquility and Drew didn't mix. Once the federal administrators had cemented their control of taxation, he warned Frost, "they will follow as a matter of course with the occupation of legislative and administrative fields as well on the ground that their over-all tax powers demand over-all administrative powers."[6] The solution, he insisted, was for Ontario and Quebec to go it alone, to harmonize their own taxation policies as much as possible to minimize competition, and to wait the federal government out.

Frost, the loyal lieutenant, did as he was told. Fortunately, the size of government was still sufficiently small, and the Ontario economy was expanding so quickly, that the federal funds weren't necessary. Ontario could, of course, have imposed its own personal income tax on top of the federal one, but both Frost and Drew agreed that this was a quick way to political oblivion. Instead, they made do with a tax on corporate profits, succession taxes (one area where the federal and provincial governments each took a bite—a testament to the lack of political power of the dead and their survivors), and liquor and gasoline taxes. As it turned out, this booty was more than enough to see Ontario through the early post-war years.

But it could not go on forever. Ontario had been transformed by the war and its technologies into a large, modern industrial state. Between 1941 and 1951, the costs of war notwithstanding, the Ontario population had grown by 800,000, to 4.6 million. Within the next five years it had grown by another 800,000, and by 1961 would be 6.2 million. The fear of depression had been swept away by the exultation of victory over fascism, and it seemed every couple's first instinct was to have babies—lots and lots of babies. The end of the war also left Europe awash in refugees and others seeking to escape the impoverished continent—especially from Italy and eastern Europe. They flooded by the hundreds of thousands across the Atlantic, many of them settling in Toronto, which eventually grew to have a larger population of Italians than most cities in Italy. At the end of the Second World War, the Ontario population was still two-thirds British. By 1960 it had dropped to one-half.

The new arrivals came in search of jobs, and jobs there were. Unemployment averaged a remarkable 2½ per cent between 1947 and 1956 in Ontario. The decimation of Europe and Asia had left the province as one of the few functioning industrial economies, even as the advances in petrochemicals, nuclear energy, aviation, automotive design, and other fields brought on by the war now became available for peacetime use. Electrification and refrigeration raised living standards in town and country, new processes in prefabricated construction made housing cheap, and advancing sewers and water mains helped spread cities into what was once countryside. Just west of Toronto G.S. Shipp and Sons constructed Applewood Acres, 850 homes and a shopping plaza in Toronto Township, and the suburban sprawl of Mississauga—a city that increased its population by twelve times between 1950 and 1985—was born. Urban planners discarded the mixed-use, grid-based city plans of Ontario's traditional cities in favour of arterial roads, strictly zoned subdivisions, and commercial plazas. Urban Ontario joined the rest of the Western hemisphere in surrendering cities to the imperatives of the automobile.

Blessed with forests and minerals to feed its economic machine, blessed with major primary industries—especially steel—to transform those resources into the raw components of manufacturing, blessed with sophisticated manufacturers capable of competitively constructing everything from airplanes to shoes, blessed in so many ways, Ontarians saw their province as the golden goose that could, in time, produce wealth almost beyond the dreams of avarice. But there were stresses. Thousands of veterans returning home from the wars needed training and housing. The province needed modern highways to connect the western, southern, and eastern borders with the industrial centre, and to bring the wealth down from the north. It needed to provide security for its population through unemployment and old age insurance, so that workers would work and consume with confidence rather than hoarding their resources as they had in the 1930s and starving the economy of cash. Most of all, Ontario desperately needed even more power: electricity, oil, gas, and, ultimately, nuclear power to fuel its industries and homes. All these needs the state was increasingly expected to meet, and Leslie Frost was convinced that succession duties and gasoline taxes would not be enough to meet them. Still, there was nothing to be done: Mackenzie King was Mackenzie King, and George Drew was George Drew. The treasurer fiddled with his books, managed as best he could, and bided his time. He didn't have to bide for long.

In 1948 George Drew, convinced it was his natural destiny to rescue Canada from the incompetence and venality of Liberal Ottawa, left the provincial stage to become leader of the federal Progressive Conservatives, where he swiftly exchanged an unbroken record of political success for one of unremitting defeat. (Provincial politicians, champions of the regional interest, have had a uniformly unsuccessful track record in federal politics.) As most expected, Leslie Miscampbell Frost handily won the convention to become Ontario's sixteenth premier. Shortly after, Mackenzie King, now prime minister of a country unrecognizable from when he first took office in 1921, finally decided his time had come and stepped down as leader. He was succeeded by the avuncular, quietly confident Louis St. Laurent. Both Ottawa and Queen's Park had new administrations. Frost determined they would also have a new relationship.

Frost was a very different man from Drew. While the imperious former colonel rushed from point A to point B—"there was always a sense of urgency with Mr. Drew"[7]—Frost preferred, literally, to put his feet up on his messy desk and invite a cabinet minister who wanted to chat to knock on the door and come in. "Well now, sir," he would say, "I look at this from the barber chair at Lindsay,"[8] the small town northeast of Toronto where he practised law and politics, and where he represented the constituents for twenty-four years. As with most political personalities, Frost's down-home affability was a mask; he ruled with a smile and an iron will. Frost liked to be called "Old Man Ontario," but his oft-defeated political enemies dubbed him "the Silver Fox." Still, success in politics for Frost meant looking for ways to reach agreement, to minimize differences, to get things done by getting along. Wars weren't his preferred method of diplomacy.

Shortly after the June 1949 federal election, in which St. Laurent handily dispatched Drew as so many Liberal prime ministers had so many Conservative opposition leaders before them, Frost sent St. Laurent a private, friendly letter, congratulating him on his victory and suggesting they meet at some convenient time with a view to establishing a more cooperative relationship. This was an extraordinary back-stab, considering that the Liberal prime minister had just defeated Frost's predecessor. But politics is the art of the necessary, and Frost had no qualms about working with St. Laurent, if it served Ontario's interest. Conveniently, the editor of the *Ottawa Journal* died shortly thereafter, giving Frost and St. Laurent a pretext for being at the same place at the same time. After the funeral service the two first ministers repaired to St. Laurent's office for fruitful discussions, which Frost then followed up on with another letter, summarizing the meeting and setting out an agenda for action. St. Laurent and his ministers, delighted, went to work.

From those meetings, and others that followed, emerged a completely new and unprecedented Queen's Park–Parliament Hill axis, one unheard of in the country's history, and one that reshaped its very fabric. From being the sovereigntist defender of central Canada, preserving its own interest in alliance with Quebec at whatever cost to the larger interest, Ontario pivoted 180 degrees. Every year the province became more comfortable within Ottawa's embrace, the old confrontations receding into, and then out of, memory. So profound was this union, so emphatic the national transformation, that at first most observers could only wonder what might have been accomplished had it started sooner.

In a series of agreements negotiated between 1949 and 1957, Ontario surrendered a broad range of taxing authority, renting it to

Ottawa in exchange for an annual per capita stipend. The deal, on its face, was no more in Ontario's interest than it had been in the past. With about 40 per cent of the population and almost 50 per cent of the gross domestic product, it would have been far more to Ontario's benefit to keep its taxes within its own borders. In 1957 Frost agreed to a national equalization program created to ensure that weaker provinces would be able to sustain national standards in health care, education, and other services. Although it would largely be paid for by Ontario taxpayers, there was little controversy. The province seemed to most people big enough for this kind of altruism. After all, as historian and economist Harold Innis had put it a generation before, "an empire has its obligations as well as its opportunities."[9]

More important, there was a *quid pro quo* in the deal, and the quo, Frost reasoned, was more than worth the quid. Most of Ontario's internal hydroelectric energy reserves had been exploited, the petroleum fields around Sarnia were rapidly being depleted, and the province lacked internal sources of natural gas. Once again, the province faced an emerging energy crisis. The time had come to build the St. Lawrence waterway, without delay. Not only would a deepwater canal open Ontario's ports from Cornwall to the Lakehead to international shipping, but the electricity produced by damming the St. Lawrence would satisfy Ontario's electrical needs for a generation. As part of the new spirit of cooperation, Ontario and Ottawa agreed in 1951 to develop the Canadian portion of the new seaway together: Ontario would be responsible for the dams and power; the federal government would handle the canals. With this agreement in hand, the St. Laurent government presented the Americans with a rare ultimatum: either agree to build the seaway, jointly and now, St. Laurent warned the American president, Dwight Eisenhower, or Canada would build it on her own. This was probably an empty threat, since an all-Canadian seaway would have been at least four times as expensive as a Canadian-American joint venture, but Eisenhower used the Canadian ultimatum to force a recalcitrant Congress to approve the project. In 1954 Canada and the United States concluded the agreement, and the St. Lawrence Seaway was under way. Five years later, on April 20, 1959, the first deepwater vessel glided through its locks.

The seaway was an awesome undertaking. Canada invested $330 million and America $130 million in the complex series of locks linking the eastern end of Lake Ontario to the river below Montreal. Lakeside communities along the north shore of the lake were inundated to create Lake St. Lawrence; 500 buildings and 6,500 people were moved from "The Lost Villages" to the newly created Long Sault and Ingleside. The seaway boosted the economies of every province and state that bordered it, lowering the cost of Quebec iron ore that now supplied the Hamilton and Sault Ste. Marie steel mills, and opening western grain to eastern exports. The railroads and Halifax paid the price. Ontario reaped the benefit of so much new power that, by the advent of the 1960s, virtually all the province's electricity was generated by water.

With Ontario's hydroelectric needs taken care of, at least for the medium term, the next pressing question was securing reliable long-term supplies of oil and natural gas, a growing source of energy for home and industry. Natural gas could be found in quantity in two places: Texas and Alberta. The province's private-sector natural gas suppliers favoured making a deal with Texas to construct a pipeline to deliver the vital fuel from the Lone Star state to Ontario, and perhaps on to Montreal. Certainly the Texans were willing, and the Albertans preferred to sell their gas south of the border anyway, so a Texas-to-Ontario and Alberta-to-the Midwest swap seemed reasonable. But it did not seem reasonable to Leslie Frost or to C.D. Howe, the federal minister of trade and commerce and the most powerful man in the country after St. Laurent—if that. Both Frost and Howe agreed that signing a deal with Texas would leave Ontario's economy vulnerable. Texas could, after all, change its mind some day and sell the natural gas to someone else. Taking the natural gas from Alberta, however, would keep it all in the family. Better still, a pipeline from Alberta to Toronto and Montreal would have to go through Ontario's north, bringing jobs and development to that still-underdeveloped region—a notion that appealed to both Frost and Howe, who represented the riding of Port Arthur. The obstacles to the deal were formidable: neither the Albertans nor the Ontario gas companies liked the idea, both believing their interests would be better served by the cross-border swap. And constructing a pipeline across northern Ontario would be horrifically expensive: the profits from sales would not likely ever repay the cost of construction. But Frost and Howe had made up their minds. When Consumers Gas cut a deal with the Americans despite opposition from the two governments, Howe arranged to have it blocked by refusing to grant a permit for the pipeline to cross the Niagara River below the falls. Whirlpools and rocks notwithstanding, the federal government blandly informed the enraged businessmen it could never countenance such an obstruction on a navigable river.

The two governments wheedled, threatened, and cajoled the reluctant private consortiums into submerging their personal interests and agreeing to create the Trans-Canada Pipelines Ltd. The federal and Ontario governments ultimately footed the bill for the northern Ontario portion of the line. As for the reluctant Albertans, Frost was standing in the room when Howe told the unhappy Ernest Manning, premier of Alberta, that Alberta would not be permitted to sell any gas to the American Midwest "unless the needs of central and eastern Canada were provided for first."[10] Pushing the pipeline deal through became such an obsession of Howe's that it brought down both him and his government. The Liberals' decision to invoke closure on the legislation to finance the deal so enraged the opposition and the public that St. Laurent lost the 1957 election. Frost was quite unhappy with the federal Conservatives for opposing the agreement, and he raised not a finger to help them in Ontario.

But the deal, and ultimately the pipeline, went through.

Much else went through during these halcyon years of the Ottawa-Ontario alliance. The two governments helped launch and fund the Trans-Canada Highway. They cooperated in developing the technology for nuclear reactors, a crucial support for Ontario's energy needs once the province had run out of sites for dams. The new era of federal-provincial cooperation started the process that ultimately created the Canada Pension Plan and a social safety net for its citizens. Ontario welcomed the federal government into every area of its jurisdiction: municipal public works, subsidized housing, welfare, and postsecondary education. It became difficult to determine where one government began and the other left off. No one cared. Ontario, under the twelve years of Frost's stewardship from 1949 to 1961, experienced the greatest growth in its history: building subway lines, skyways, four-lane highways, new universities, a seaway, and thousands upon thousands of houses. The province's gross domestic product rose from $56 billion to $84 billion, in constant 1992 dollars, over the course of the decade. Growth averaged 4.3 per cent annually. All this good news, it seemed, was made possible because the provincial and the federal governments finally decided to get along. It wasn't simply that, of course, at least not entirely. Much of what the two governments created together they could have created separately, and the impetus to creation was simply a product of the times. But it was a moot point, and who really would have believed that the federal Liberals would have pushed themselves literally to their own destruction to ensure that the industrial heartland would always have its own supply of cheap Alberta gas?

There were costs, however—hidden at the time, but inevitable—and they had to be paid. John Robarts, Frost's successor, would be the first to pay them.

In 1953 the governor general, Vincent Massey, invited Leslie Frost to Rideau Hall for a dinner in honour of Dwight Eisenhower. The food was in the finest continental tradition, the wines were French, and the refined governor general, the good-natured American president, and the informal Ontario premier enjoyed each other's company. Later in the evening, Eisenhower took Frost by the shoulder and began rhapsodizing about Canada. The country had great possibilities, he said, especially its water resources. The American president lamented the fact that most of his country's great rivers had become polluted. It got Frost to thinking, and eventually to creating the Ontario Water Resources Commission. He selected a young backbencher, John Robarts, to run it. The appointment marked the beginning of the political rise of the MPP from London. When Frost decided to step down, in 1961, Robarts, now education minister, entered the race to succeed him, winning on the sixth ballot.

"I'm a management man myself," Robarts once said. "This is the era of the management man ... I'm a complete product of the times."[11] He was its product in other ways as well. Though he lacked John Kennedy's political charisma, Robarts was very much part of the Kennedy generation: a hard-drinking, fast-living, womanizing, driven man who believed that everything in life, including government, should be big and bold. The only premier of Ontario born outside the province, John Parmenter Robarts was the son of a bank manager who moved around the country as new posts presented themselves. Robarts was born in Banff, Alberta, in 1917, arriving in his teens in London, Ontario, a city that remained his base for the rest of his life. Like Kennedy, he served in the navy as a lieutenant, and was mentioned in dispatches at the Battle of Salerno. He belonged to that generation of men who came of age in depression and war, who returned from overseas older than their years, and who were convinced that no human endeavour was impossible, given sufficient determination and organization. These men built the world we live in today.

Robarts inherited a provincial government in transition. Although Leslie Frost had inaugurated the great program of expansion that transformed Ontario into a modern industrial state, its social programs retained many of their pre-war features. Most people, for instance, continued to rely on private health insurance; the education system contained both new comprehensive schools and old, one-room school houses. Frost had launched North America's first regional government by joining the suburbs surrounding Toronto with the city to create Metropolitan Toronto, but much of the rest of the province remained fragmented in local governments already diagnosed by experts as too small and parochial to handle the challenges of urban Ontario society. The Ontario bureaucracy itself, although it had grown from 13,685 in 1950 to 32,302 in 1960, retained a provincial quality, its membership more comfortable with the ledgers of the pre-war era than the new computers that were already beginning to reshape work and the workplace.

The truly provincial quality of the Ontario public service was brought forcibly home to Robarts in the negotiations that led up to the establishment of the Canada Pension Plan. Pensions, like most social policy, nominally fell within provincial jurisdiction. Ontario had launched a public pension plan administered by private insurers in the 1950s. But the federal government was anxious to secure provincial support for a national and entirely public plan, and the new Liberal prime minister, Lester B. Pearson, called a federal-provincial conference for July 1963 to discuss the matter. He was also interested in launching a new loan fund to aid municipal development, yet another area that was supposed to be exclusively a provincial jurisdiction.

While Robarts was interested in ensuring that pensions were portable—that they could be carried from one plan to another when a resident moved around the country—he had not signed on to the notion of a federal plan. Quebec, openly hostile to federal intrusion in its jurisdiction, was at work on a comprehensive plan of its own. The Quebec government had never surrendered, as Ontario had, its control over taxation and social policy during the 1950s. Indeed, its determination to resist federal domination was all the fiercer, now that nationalist flames were fuelling its idealist youth. The new Quebec premier, Jean Lesage, presided over a militant and restless society that was shaking off the strictures of its quasi-feudal, theocratic past and modernizing with a vengeance. In a move reminiscent of the old Ontario-Quebec axis, both Lesage and Robarts sharply criticized the federal proposals at the conference. On the municipal front, they demanded that any federal money for municipalities flow through and be controlled by the provincial governments.

Lester Pearson, himself a quintessential "management man," had been present at the creation of the Canadian foreign service in the 1930s. He had risen through its ranks until he shifted smoothly to the cabinet table and to a Nobel Peace Price for his help in brokering an end to the Suez Crisis. After taking a drubbing from the erratic but engaging John Diefenbaker in 1958, Pearson had rebuilt the Liberal Party and returned it to power, albeit as a minority government, in 1963. He came to office imbued with the mandarin's conviction that the knottiest problem could be unravelled if men of good will were prepared to compromise. Anxious to establish a new spirit of "cooperative federalism," he agreed on the municipal front. On pensions, however, consensus was impossible. Lesage made it clear he was unlikely to support any national scheme; Quebec would go it alone. While Robarts was prepared to consider a national plan, he announced that it must fit with Ontario's existing plan. The conference adjourned, and Robarts and federal health minister Judy LaMarsh got into a slanging match that helped Robarts win the next provincial election.

Ultimately, however, the Ontario premier couldn't resist his own constituents' desire for a national, portable, dependable pension plan. In an attempt to co-opt Quebec and do an end-run around

Ontario, Pearson agreed to a federal-provincial first ministers' conference in Quebec City to discuss pensions at the end of March 1964. It was a disastrous mistake for the federal leader. As a foretaste of the ugliness to come, demonstrations marred the conference, and security was so heavy that most first ministers were unable to venture outside their hotel rooms when not at the conference. As the meeting progressed, it became clear to everyone that the Quebec plan that Lesage had already unveiled was vastly superior to the one proposed by the federal government. "Maybe we should contract into the Quebec plan," Pearson joked,[12] and essentially that's what the federal government did, modelling the Canada Pension Plan on the best features of the Quebec scheme. Robarts, outflanked, went along.

The pension plan debate brought home two truths to the Ontario premier. The first was that his public service lacked the managerial expertise of its federal counterpart (which was itself not as sophisticated as the Quebec bureaucracy). Robarts immediately set about modernizing and expanding the province's public administration. Within a decade it would grow from 30,000 to 70,000 members. But the premier realized something more: the federal government had abandoned its policy of tailoring its policies and priorities to Ontario's needs. Quebec was now the focus of federal intentions, with Ontario watching from the sidelines. The province had surrendered its sovereignty with the understanding that Ottawa would tend to its agenda. But Frost had no sooner negotiated the entente than it had begun to erode. Squabbles over taxes between Frost and Diefenbaker had forced Ontario to implement its first-ever sales tax in 1961. Now, although not actively hostile to Ontario, Pearson was obviously fixated on Quebec, as the federal government tried to placate the new militancy of the French nation. Ontario, it was clear, was expected to go along. Since it had already surrendered much of its autonomy, it had little choice.

How seriously Ontario's ability to protect its interests had been compromised became obvious in 1965, when Pearson, having failed at his second attempt at winning a majority government, decided to do an about-face in federal-provincial relations. Gone was the brief era of cooperative federalism. Ottawa would counter Quebec City by asserting its authority. Its most crucial counter-offensive was in the area of health care. Most provinces, including Ontario, had some form of plan to help lower-income residents pay for visits to the doctor or the hospital, and Robarts had also passed legislation capping the maximum rate of contributions to private sector medical insurance. But in 1962 the Saskatchewan government launched Canada's first fully public Medicare plan—the creation of its former premier, Tommy Douglas—providing all citizens with virtually identical access to most forms of health treatment. Pearson decided that Saskatchewan's plan should be extended nationwide. In July 1965 he proposed a shared-cost national Medicare plan, based on the principles of universal access, portability, comprehensiveness, and government administration. Robarts harshly attacked both the plan and Ottawa's refusal to consult with the provinces before proposing it. The Ontario government, he was convinced, could never afford to fund such a program, especially with the federal government dominating so much of the tax field. Pearson, gambling that popular pressure would force Robarts and the other premiers to adopt the plan whether they wanted to or not, pushed through the legislation, to take effect on July 1, 1968.

For more than a year Robarts held out, sticking with the Ontario plan while accusing the federal program of "tampering improperly with matters which are directly the responsibility of the province,"[13] even as he and other premiers lobbied Ottawa to surrender some of its income-tax power. Pearson and his finance minister, Mitchell Sharp, were unmoved. If you can't afford the program, raise your taxes, Sharp told the pleading premiers. Worse, to help finance the federal portion of the program, Ottawa announced it was discontinuing funding to other shared-cost programs, principally in the areas of postsecondary education and training. This, it would turn out, was a very thin edge of a very large wedge. The federal government had discovered a powerful tool for imposing uniform social programs across the country: introduce the program, offering to share the costs with the provinces, count on public pressure to force the provincial governments to adopt the program, then, once it is entrenched, reduce or eliminate federal funding, leaving the provinces to sustain the program while moving on to the next proposal. It worked. Under mounting public pressure, Robarts surrendered: on October 1, 1968, Ontario joined the national Medicare program with its Ontario Health Insurance Program. To pay for it, Treasurer Charles MacNaughton revealed during his March 1969 budget address that the provincial government would implement its own personal income tax on top of the federal tax. The fight over who would occupy which part of the tax field had ended simply by enlarging the field. Voters appeared to accept the tax increase as a necessary substitute for medical insurance premiums.

Yet the Ontario-Ottawa entente, if stricken, was by no means dead. Robarts, though he complained about and sometimes bristled at the growing apathy of the federal power towards the heartland, never contemplated rebellion the way Quebec did. And in the mid-1960s Ottawa proved, once again, that it had formidable resources available to advance Ontario's cause and was prepared to use them. The American and Canadian federal governments jointly negotiated the Automotive Products Trade Agreement, commonly known as the Auto Pact, in which all automobiles manufactured in either country were exempt from duty in the other, within certain limits that were, as it turned out, to Canada's economic benefit. The Auto Pact was more an example of managed trade than free trade, but it would powerfully lift and sustain Ontario's manufacturing base, bolstering automobile manufacturing as well as auto parts (largely Canadian-owned). Decades later, it would offer a Canadian-made conduit for

America's Japanese rivals to enter the North American auto manufacturing centre, and would be used—although the precedent was imperfect—as an example of the virtues of free trade.

But if the province and its premier were grateful for the blessings the Auto Pact provided Ontario's economy, the federation as a whole was in a dismal state as it prepared to celebrate Canada's Centennial in 1967—the one hundredth anniversary of Confederation. The constitution remained ensconced in Westminster, although the federal government had amended it unilaterally in 1949, affirming its power to amend the constitution in areas of exclusively federal jurisdiction without provincial consent and making the Supreme Court the final court of appeal. Mowat would have fought it to the death; Frost just shrugged. Now Quebec militancy and federal intransigence wrecked a bid to celebrate the Centennial by repatriating the constitution with a new amending formula. Extreme Quebec separatists were less interested in constitutional renewal than in bombing post office boxes. The new Quebec premier, Daniel Johnson, demanded a level of internal autonomy for his province that would make it virtually a sovereign state within the federation. Robarts, convinced that misunderstanding was at the root of the rot, convened his own Confederation of Tomorrow Conference, a forum for first ministers to discuss the future of Canada. The conference would not only provide Johnson with an opportunity to explain renascent Quebec to the rest of Canada, Robarts reasoned, but, as it invaded Ottawa's jurisdictional domain, nicely pay back the federal government for its string of slights. A 1966 federal-provincial conference that was supposed to have presented a renewed federation in time for the Centennial ended in such discord over Ottawa's refusal to surrender more tax room to the provinces that a final communiqué could not even be drafted. If Ottawa would not bend to preserve the federation, Robarts reasoned, Ontario would lead the way.

Prime Minister Pearson, incensed at the idea of a province

convening a federal-provincial conference, stayed away from the Confederation of Tomorrow. But Johnson and most of the other premiers did show up, and on November 27, 1967, the conference convened on the top floor of the grand new black steel and glass skyscraper, the Toronto-Dominion Centre, the tallest building in the country and a symbol of Toronto's dominance over the world of finance. Although most observers, and most premiers, were shocked by Johnson's call for total sovereignty over all economic and social policy within his province's borders, everyone had a grand old time rubbishing Ottawa, and the conference was pronounced an enormous success. It probably never occurred to Robarts that Ontario was as much to blame as the federal government for Quebec's alienation. Throughout most of Confederation, the two provincial governments had stood side by side, frustrating or at least limiting federal incursions into provincial rights. Then Ontario had abandoned Quebec and sold its political soul for the sake of hydro power and natural gas, leaving Quebecers feeling alienated and alone amid an English conspiracy. Had Ontario preserved the Ontario-Quebec axis, it might well have helped contain, or at least soften, the spirit of nationalism that first inflamed Quebec in the 1960s. But, by the time of the Centennial, that old alliance was already a dissipating memory.

The Ontario Conservatives attributed their longevity to their foresight in changing leaders at the right time. Facing the inevitable, and also a body that had started to rebel against his freewheeling lifestyle, John Robarts announced his retirement from politics in 1971. It had been a good run. If the provincial government had lost power relative to Ottawa, in absolute terms it had never been more influential. The Robarts regime had reorganized and reformed the province's education system, expanded its welfare program (with federal assistance), largely completed its highway infrastructure, modernized its hospital system, and reorganized municipal governments. Robarts had commanded a national stage in fighting for national unity, and he would go on to co-chair a national task force on unity before his depression after suffering a stroke caused him to commit suicide in 1982.

Robarts had inherited Frost's legacy of surrendering autonomy in exchange for federal favours, but the favours had been few and the autonomy was surrendered grudgingly. Ontario's seventeenth premier spent much of his time in office attempting to cope with an autocratic and distracted federal government little interested in Ontario's demands, determined instead to pursue a national agenda that, in reality, meant placating Quebec while imposing its will on the rest of the country. This strategy had long worked, provided Ontario had been placated too. But now Ottawa appeared to be less and less interested in favouring its largest province, leaving the premier with neither the powers of the pre-war premiers nor the special treatment accorded his predecessor. Still, the Ontario voter appeared not to notice or to care. It mattered not where the program came from, so long as it arrived. As for taxes, well, they were taxes and just went up like everything else, including the cost of lettuce. Ontario was still in the heyday of its role as the heartland of a great federation centred in Ottawa, troubled only by French Canadian militancy. One politician, William Grenville Davis, presided over the Indian summer of that union.

"Does Ontario exist?"[14] a social critic asked in 1968, and it was a fair question. The province had transformed itself in the space of twenty years from the imperial centre of a loose federation to the heartland of something that, at times, resembled a nation-state. Up until the Second World War the province had dominated the federation, commanding the heights of population and industry, unashamedly aggressive in pursuing its economic and political self-interest, grandiose in its determination to influence the rest of the country, especially in the West, suspicious of any attempt by the federal government to impose a national will on its turf. Since the war, however, power had been surrendered, handed over to Ottawa in exchange for its literal counterpart—hydroelectric power and fossil fuels—and Ontario had gradually submerged its political identity until it seemed to disappear altogether. When Ontarians looked for leaders who would protect the province's interests, they increasingly looked to Ottawa. It was Ottawa that led the fight to provide them with the social services they sought—pensions, unemployment insurance, health care, access to higher education, social assistance, subsidized housing. It was Ottawa that trumpeted the beautiful dream of a free, united, bilingual, and multicultural people living together happily from sea to sea; Ottawa that confronted and sought to contain the dangerous aspirations of restless Quebec. The Ontario government appeared to be, at best, a conduit for federal programs, and, at worst, a spoke in the wheel, resisting Medicare and squabbling over provincial rights. No wonder, then, that Ontarians increasingly came to equate the national interest, as espoused by their national governments, with their own interests. The two were synonymous, and both sides knew it.

In fact, the so-called national social programs were only national because Ontario embraced them. When it became clear that the Quebec government was determined to retain control over everything from pensions to welfare, the Pearson administration invented the "opting out" compromise. A province could opt out of a proposed program and still receive full funding, provided its own program matched the federal one. Opting out conveniently allowed Ottawa to launch national programs throughout English Canada, while Quebec went its own, but similar, way. But opting out worked only if Ontario never opted out. If both central Canadian provinces had insisted on retaining control over social spending, the programs would have had no pretense of being national at all. They would simply be regional programs sponsored by the federal government to provide the peripheral provinces with services similar to those enjoyed by central Canada—equalization programs in fact, if not in name. But Ontario never opted out. Though Robarts resisted Medicare, denouncing it as "a Machiavellian scheme ... one of the greatest frauds that has ever been perpetrated on the people of this country,"[15] he submitted to the federal will within a year. In all other cases, Ontario opted in to federal programs immediately, making them "national," at least within the English nation.

In some ways Ontario simply ceased to be. While to regional eyes—the Albertan farmer, the Newfoundland fisher—the province still seemed domineering, Ontarians virtuously regarded themselves as paragons of the national interest, the truest Canadians. Did their equalization payments not help build Nova Scotia universities and Saskatchewan roads? Did their corporate and personal taxes not subsidize economic development schemes in Cape Breton? Did their ready support for the Canada Assistance Plan not ensure that welfare would be available in Winnipeg as readily as in Toronto? Albertans might think of themselves as Albertans, Prince Edward Islanders might celebrate the Island Way, but Ontarians were Canadians first of all.

Immigration had a lot to do with it. In most parts of Canada the population was largely descended from those who first arrived there. Nova Scotia in 1968 was remarkably similar demographically to the way it had been a century earlier, its population largely composed of descendants of the original settlers or of new arrivals from Great Britain, its definable motherland. Demographic insularity helped preserve the provincial culture, its sense of history, its links to the past. But Ontario had been inundated since the Second World War by immigrants from southern and eastern Europe, and then increasingly from Asia and the Caribbean. Although rural Ontario still retained some of the flavour of nineteenth-century Upper Canada, Toronto, especially, had become one of the most racially mixed cities in the world. The new arrivals injected an exciting cosmopolitanism into the city, with little Italy, little Portugal, and Chinatown turning the downtown into a United Nations of neighbourhoods. But they also served to obscure, and even obliterate, its settler culture. Mostly, this change was for the good. For more than a century the Orange Lodge had exerted its baleful influence on the province's politics, sharpening tensions between Protestants and Catholics, sustaining ancient rivalries of race and religion. By 1968 it was a spent force. Protestant-Catholic tension seemed ludicrous in a society whose middle-class youth were delving into the spiritual mysteries of Buddhism and marijuana. Old Ontario was in a nursing home; George Brown was a question in a history test, and history was an optional course. The early history was submerged beneath the dynamic, multicultural polyglot of the Golden Horseshoe, the nearly unbroken band of urban housing and commerce that surrounded the eastern end of Lake Ontario from Oshawa to Niagara Falls. "The contours of the Ontario mind are formed by deep valleys carved into a flat surface, rather than by a collection of jagged hills and other leading projections," one historian opined.[16] Even at that, he was being charitable.

The submergence was literal. The landmark historic sites of the War of 1812, the farm fields that had launched and sustained its early economy, the downtowns that were its mercantile and industrial centre were lost in a sea of asphalt and concrete, as Hamilton merged with Burlington merged with Oakville merged with Mississauga, Toronto, Pickering, Ajax, Whitby, and Oshawa. The province's population had exploded in the 1960s by 1.5 million people, to 7.7 million. Many of them were young, products of the legendary baby boom, and they crammed the province's new universities, demonstrated on its campuses, and hung out at Rochdale College and in Yorkville, heart of the hippie movement. Otherwise, blandness predominated, in cookie-cutter suburbs and monotonous office blocks, apartment buildings, malls, and plazas. Years of American economic encroachment, aided by high tariffs, had turned the province into "(Canada) Inc.": the centre of a branch-plant economy that made nothing particularly Canadian, but much that was useful. Nationalist critics bemoaned, but there were always the Canada Council for the Arts and the Ontario Arts Council to fund the Stratford and Shaw festivals, along with the new publishing houses sustained as much by government grants as reader interest.

Over this amorphous, featureless, prosperous suburban expanse, William Grenville Davis presided as premier from 1971 to 1984. They were some of the most tumultuous years in Canada's history, the years of the oil crisis and separatism, of economic crisis and international intrigue. You wouldn't have known it if you had lived at Queen's Park. Bill Davis was famously bland: the pipe-smoking personification of 1970s Ontario; the product of a small town that had become a sprawling suburb of Toronto; a politician who, as education minister, had implemented a new curriculum that emphasized self-worth over rote learning; a so-called Conservative who launched a public television broadcaster, TV Ontario, and bought part of an oil company; a leader who avoided controversy and confrontation above all, and who demonstrated, often successfully, that the best way to achieve consensus was simply to delay. "It is not the responsibility of government to entertain," he maintained.[17]

During the Davis government, the entente between Queen's Park and Parliament Hill reached its apogee. Under Frost, Ontario had surrendered its taxing power in exchange for access to electricity and fuel. Under Robarts, Ontario had surrendered control over social policy, but was compensated by the Auto Pact. Under Davis, power would again dominate the agenda. As oil-induced economic shocks rumbled through the Western industrial economies, threatening to topple them, Ontario looked to Ottawa to protect its industries by securing cheap oil from Alberta. In exchange, Davis became Pierre Trudeau's loyal and unquestioning ally, as Canada's most imperious prime minister sought to restructure both the Canadian Constitution and the Canadian economy.

In many ways, Davis and Trudeau were opposites: the premier a slightly pudgy and professionally avuncular champion of the middle of the road, who never wore a tie that anyone could describe; the prime minister the living embodiment of statesman as ruthless aesthete, who could quote Baudelaire one day and face down a rag-tag band of terrorists in Quebec the next, and who waged mortal combat with separatist forces in Quebec even as he pointedly ignored much of the rest of the country. Yet the two got along famously, for the simple reason that they shared similar visions of the country: Canada, for them, was, or should be, a modern, post-industrial, bilingual, powerfully centralized state, dominated by a great French and a great English province, with the regions treated as laboratories in economic development theory. Their alliance would often be tested, and would emerge stronger as a series of economic and constitutional storms washed over the country.

The OPEC crisis arrived in the wake of the 1973 Arab-Israeli War, when the members of the Organization of Petroleum Exporting Countries, partly to avenge American support for Israel, announced their intention to manage and restrict the supplies of oil to the West. The price of oil quadrupled in a space of three months. There could be few jurisdictions more potentially vulnerable to the impact of the oil shocks than Ontario. The province's manufacturing economy relied heavily on oil and natural gas. Its export economy relied on the economic health of the United States, which was under assault from all sides, partly due to its calamitous policy of financing the Vietnam War through inflation. The mainstay of Ontario's manufacturing sector, the auto industry, was affected both by the petroleum shortage and by growing Japanese and German competition, as the wartime losers again emerged as powerful competitors. Ontario was a rust belt waiting to happen.

There was little Canada could do about the American economy and the overseas threats, but it could do something about oil. Canada was largely self-sufficient in petroleum, although, because of distribution problems, Alberta exported oil while the Maritimes and Quebec imported it. Ontario relied on Alberta oil; if it rose to world prices, Ontario would be paying world prices along with everybody else. But Ontario didn't have to be like everybody else. Bill Davis hardly had to press; Finance Minister Marc Lalonde, in many ways an intellectual mirror of the prime minister, though without the charm, knew the impact world oil prices would have on the country's industrial heartland. Besides, there were more votes and many more Liberals in Ontario than in the West. As prices rose, the federal government swiftly instituted export controls and regulations that protected Ontario industry at the West's expense. Alberta and Saskatchewan were forced to sell their oil to Ontario at below-market prices. Further, the federal government slapped a tax on oil exports, using the money to subsidize the cost of oil imports for the East, while attempting to wrest responsibility for oil exploration and development away from the western provinces. The Albertans reacted with rage. "Let the Eastern bastards freeze in the dark," their bumper stickers read. Trudeau, in his arrogance and his desire to protect central Canada's manufacturing centre, had created a second centre of alienation. From 1973 on, the West's discontents would be only slightly less strident than Quebec's.

The second shock—both to the West and to Confederation—came in 1979, with a fresh round of oil-price increases in the wake of the overthrow of the Shah of Iran. Canadian oil prices had finally begun to rise to world levels, and the minority Conservative government of Alberta-based Joe Clark promised to allow the trend to continue. The Conservatives, however, foolishly let themselves be defeated over their budget in the House of Commons. A revitalized Trudeau campaigned in part on a platform of protecting Canadian industry from the oil shocks by providing a "made-in-Canada" oil policy. He won, and then set about making policy with a vengeance. On October 28, 1980, the Trudeau government unveiled its new National Energy Program, "a more complex, sweeping and breathtaking policy initiative than any ever placed before Parliament."[18] The NEP was more than an energy policy: it was a blatant attempt to reshape the energy sector by nationalizing parts of it, expelling American interests in the rest, and increasing federal control over everything. Through a mixture of regulations and incentives, it shifted oil exploration out of the provincially controlled Alberta oilfields and into the federally controlled "Canada Lands" of the Arctic and Atlantic seabeds, and encouraged the state-owned Petro-Canada and other Canadian petroleum companies to take over the foreign competition. To ice the cake, the powers of the Foreign Investment Review Agency were stiffened, with an eye to reversing American domination of Canadian industry.

The anger of westerners, especially Albertans, over the NEP rivalled that of Quebec at the hanging of Louis Riel a century before. As Riel's hanging destroyed the Conservative Party in Quebec, so the NEP destroyed the Liberal Party in the Prairie provinces. For the rest of the century the Liberals would depend for their support principally on the two provinces of central Canada, while the West spun dangerously close to escaping Confederation's orbit. But the evil genius of the NEP was that it enraged Atlantic Canada as well as the West. The incentives for offshore exploration in the Atlantic offered a potential economic boon to Newfoundland, Canada's poorest and most dependent province, especially when the rich Hibernia oilfield was discovered. Hibernia also offered the promise of increased revenues for the Newfoundland government's coffers, provided the provincial government was offered joint ownership and control of the oilfields. But the seabed is federal territory, and Trudeau quickly made it clear to Brian Peckford, Newfoundland's premier, that Ottawa intended to retain exclusive jurisdiction over the oil. The Supreme Court of Canada backed him up by ruling in 1984 that the natural resources of the offshore region were exclusively federal domain. The federal intransigence soon had Peckford talking like a separatist as well. Nova Scotia, which also had potential access to major oilfields, was almost as unhappy.

The West was apoplectic, Atlantic Canada in a fury. In Quebec the separatist and anti-Trudeau Parti Québécois, which had come to power in 1976, had lost the 1980 referendum on sovereignty, but been re-elected the following year. All of Canada was up in arms. Only Ontario remained loyal, and her loyalty was unshakable. Everything Trudeau had done in the name of Canada was in reality done in the name of Ontario. Davis had openly urged the federal bureaucrats to force Alberta to sell its oil and gas domestically at below-market prices in the 1970s. "The federal government must use its influence and constitutional authority to direct oil and natural gas revenue flows in accordance with agreed national objectives,"[19] he had maintained. When Joe Clark signalled his intention in 1979 to end the two-tier pricing system, Davis strongly protested, damning it as "an excessive and imprudent response to the claims of the producing provinces and the petroleum industry."[20] During the 1980 federal election, in which Clark, a fellow Progressive Conservative, was fighting for his political life against a resurgent Trudeau and the Ontario seats were certain to determine the outcome, Davis went on vacation.

Ironically, the Ontario-centric federal energy policy was probably, in the end, as bad for Ontario as it was for Alberta and Newfoundland. When oil prices skyrocketed in 1973 and again in 1979, other Western nations, including the United States, accepted the inevitable and adapted their industries and consumer habits to practise conservation, switch to alternative sources of power, and buy smaller automobiles, all of which resulted in reduced energy consumption and greater efficiency. Subsidized oil and gas in Ontario allowed industries to carry on without facing up to the major investments needed to wean themselves off their dependence on cheap energy. At the same time, wages rose to absorb whatever competitive advantage lower energy costs might have provided, leaving its industries outdated and uncompetitive, ripe for a pummelling should the playing field ever even out again.

The NEP was probably the greatest failure of economic policy ever perpetrated by a federal government. Not only did it alienate both western and Atlantic Canada, and dangerously insulate Ontario from the needed disciplines of the market, but it failed by its own standards. The whole program was predicated on the assumption of high and rising energy prices. But the 1980s were barely under way when energy prices began to decline. The OPEC nations, several of whom were at war with each other, couldn't maintain the needed solidarity of purpose, and, even if they had, the energy crisis had brought major new sources of petroleum onstream, from the North Sea to the Alberta tarsands. Without high prices, offshore exploration made no economic sense. The Canadian companies that had taken advantage of the NEP incentives found themselves bleeding from uneconomical exploration costs and debt from takeovers. The Americans, infuriated by the NEP and the restrictions of the Foreign Investment Review Agency, were in no mood to exempt Canada from the rising tide of protectionism sweeping into Congress. In the end, the policy was a disaster.

But what mattered as far as the Ontario government was concerned was that Ottawa, unequivocally, was governing in Ontario's interest, at least in the field of energy. And favours offered meant favours returned. Despite Trudeau's flirtation with a constitutional policy as potentially catastrophic for national unity as his National Energy Program, he received Davis's unconditional loyalty as he sought to wrest the Canadian Constitution from Westminster, without, if need be, provincial consent.

At first Trudeau, like his predecessor, Pearson, attempted to co-opt the provinces through conciliation. In the negotiations that led up to the Victoria Conference in 1970, Trudeau offered to surrender much of the control the federal government had assumed over social policy through its direct and shared-cost programs. Nine out of ten provinces agreed, but so tense was the situation in Quebec that nothing short of total abdication by the federal government in all fields of provincial jurisdiction would have satisfied Premier Robert Bourassa. In truth, perhaps nothing could have satisfied him. With the arrival of René Lévesque and the Parti Québécois in 1976, Trudeau, like Pearson, increasingly came to feel that he had given too much away to the provinces and that it was time to reassert the federal will. "There was a slippage of Canada towards, is it a community of communities or is it ten quasi autonomous states?" Trudeau ruminated in 1981. "That slippage has been going on for perhaps a couple of decades now and I feel that they've had to be reversed."[21] Many would argue with Trudeau's assessment that the federal government had been losing control of the agenda through the 1960s and 1970s—Medicare? the Canada Assistance Plan? grants to municipalities and postsecondary education?—but some critics reasoned that the provinces' power to opt out of programs, and to administer programs to which they opted in, had increased their role and visibility at federal expense. More to the point, the assessment reflected the centralist, statist preoccupation of Trudeau with strengthening the federal power. The National Energy Program was, at root, simply one element in his campaign to assert the economic primacy of the federal government within Confederation. The constitutional plan of 1980 was an attempt to restore political primacy.

After the defeat of the Parti Québécois referendum on sovereignty in 1980—a defeat occasioned in part by Trudeau's personal pledge to the people of Quebec that he would offer them "a new deal" within Confederation—a subdued Lévesque joined the provincial premiers in a fresh round of constitutional discussions. Trudeau was determined to patriate the constitution, while at the same time enshrining a Bill of Rights and acquiring new economic powers for the federal government. Lacking provincial agreement, he went on television on October 2, 1980, to announce that the federal government would unilaterally seek to patriate the constitution, in essence to write one by itself. The new constitution would both centralize authority and, at the same time, advance the rights of central Canada. An American-style Charter of Rights and Freedoms would supersede the provincial responsibility for civil rights; a proposed economic union to outlaw non-tariff barriers among provinces would further bolster access by Ontario's manufacturers to Canadian markets; and the proposed amending formula would provide both Ontario and Quebec with a veto. Not since John A. Macdonald had a prime minister so boldly attempted to strip the provinces of their powers without their consent.

While other provinces reacted with enraged incredulity, Ontario's Bill Davis promptly announced his wholehearted support for the constitutional plan. Ontario had now evolved about as far as was possible from the compact theory of Confederation that its own pre-war premiers had enunciated and defended. While many aspects of the new patriated constitution would have served Ontario's interests, no pre-war premier would ever have surrendered Ontario's right to veto the patriation in the first place. The other provinces, of course, remained determined to fight for their ancient liberties. They appealed to the courts and their plea was heard: on September 28, 1981, a divided Supreme Court of Canada ruled that the government had a legal right to proceed unilaterally, but that convention and "the federal spirit" required it to obtain the consent of "a substantial number" of provinces. The ruling prompted yet another round of intense negotiations, during which Attorney General Jean Chrétien, Ontario Attorney General Roy McMurtry, and Saskatchewan Attorney General Roy Romanow concocted a compromise that Trudeau and all the English-speaking premiers could accept. Lévesque, betrayed by the back-room deal from which he was excluded, ordered Quebec flags lowered to half mast when Queen Elizabeth II signed the Constitution Act, 1982, into law on the steps of Parliament.

The new constitution protected most of the traditional rights of the provinces under the old act. A proposed economic union was watered down—preserving the smaller provinces' right to support their own fledgling industries with buy-local government procurement policies—and, in a reversal of the federal power of disallowance, the provinces were given the power to enact laws that violated the provisions of the Charter of Rights and Freedoms by invoking what came to be known as the notwithstanding clause. Ontario and Quebec also lost their absolute veto; most amendments to the constitution required the consent of seven provinces making up half the population. But while Lévesque seethed at his province's humiliation, Davis beamed. The province could live with a few compromises for the sake of a constitution that, Ontarians hoped, would finally end the squabbling.

Except it didn't, of course. Every deal Davis made with his ally Trudeau would come back to haunt his province. Subsidized oil served as a debilitating drug for Ontario industry; the constitution failed to satisfy Quebec or the other provinces; and Trudeau's high-handed nationalism provoked an American backlash, prompting Brian Mulroney, Trudeau's successor, to seek full free trade to avoid the punishment of a tariff wall. Worst of all, having sold its soul to the federal government, Ontario found itself without allies among the provinces when the tables turned in Ottawa.

In some ways, Bill Davis was hostage to events outside his control. The oil crisis left Ontario dependent on an expansionist Alberta. Only the federal government could rein in the emerging giant and protect Ontario's primacy within Confederation. The West grew so fast in the 1970s, and generated so much money from oil and gas revenues, that Ontario at one point was in danger of becoming a have-not province under the equalization formula. To prevent the humiliation, the formula was rejigged so the province could continue its time-honoured role of subsidizing at least the rest of Canada outside Alberta and British Columbia. The loss of Quebec would have had terrible consequences for Ontario, but Ontario had already betrayed the Ontario-Quebec axis and had to rely on Ottawa to protect the Confederation. The Ontario government, in short, had no levers of its own left to influence the rest of the federation. Only Ottawa was available to bring the other regions into line. Ontario needed allies, but Ottawa was now the only ally available. And the Ontario population had become so thoroughly fixated on Ottawa, so completely immersed in the rhetoric of "the national interest," that the virtual merger of identities between the provincial and the federal government seemed natural, almost instinctive.

But it was not natural or instinctive. It was the product of thirty years of accommodation that itself was the reversal of more than eighty years of independence. And Davis's successors would painfully learn that Frost's forebears had guarded the province's rights and independence for a reason. Ottawa was a fickle ally, and the heartland would soon find itself confronted with a hostile prime minister now allied with Quebec and the regions. Weakened and vulnerable, Ontario would be forced to stand alone.

5

Failures and Betrayals

The tumult over the energy crisis, Quebec separatism, and the new constitution consumed and exhausted the politicians who wrestled with this seemingly ungovernable country throughout the 1970s and early 1980s. Pierre Trudeau, with the Constitution Act, 1982, promulgated and his reputation for economic mismanagement entrenched, took a walk in the February 1984 snow and decided to retire. He was succeeded, briefly, by John Turner, his former finance minister, who had left the government in a huff and returned with his ego intact, but his political skills seriously tarnished. He, in turn, succumbed in the 1984 general election to Brian Mulroney, a big-jawed, charmingly opportunistic Irish Quebec corporate lawyer who devastated the Liberals, winning majorities in every region of the country and reducing the "natural governing party" to 40 seats in the 281-seat House of Commons. In Quebec, Trudeau's nemesis, René Lévesque, left the stage as well, to be succeeded by Pierre-Marc Johnson, a man more interested in developing Québécois economic independence than political sovereignty. That same year the Parti Québécois lost power to the Liberals under Robert Bourassa, who, in a remarkable political renaissance, returned to power nine years after he had lost it in 1976. Peter Lougheed, having presided over the greatest economic boom and state expansion in Alberta's history, also stepped down, to be replaced by a genial but unimpressive Don Getty. Richard Hatfield, the loyal junior ally to Pierre Trudeau and Bill Davis in the constitution wars, lost every single seat in the provincial election in 1987, beset by personal scandal and New Brunswick's chronic economic weakness. In Saskatchewan, voters had already shown little gratitude for Peter Blakeney's efforts to help broker the constitutional compromise, throwing out the NDP in 1982 in favour of the Conservatives under Grant Devine. The NDP in Manitoba under Howard Pawley gave way to the Conservatives under Gary Filmon. In British Columbia, Bill Bennett, son of former premier W.A.C. "Wacky" Bennett, was succeeded by the far wackier Bill Vander Zalm. It seemed as though the entire political leadership of the nation had collectively desired or been compelled to hand the country over to a new crowd.

Ontario's Conservatives had always prided themselves on changing leaders at just the right time, before they became a liability to the party. Regular rotation, went the theory, revived the party from within and in the eyes of the public. Leslie Frost had governed for twelve years before making way for John Robarts, who managed the estate for a decade before handing it on to Bill Davis. Davis had presided over two majority and two minority governments, had weathered the energy crisis, the constitution crisis, and two recessions, and was considered unbeatable. "The nonstop hegemony of the Progressive Conservatives from 1942 to 1985 would be the envy of any totalitarian regime in its duration and its dutiful and lopsided legislative majorities,"[1] one analyst concluded. But Davis, who knew his history, decided to ignore the pleadings of his advisers that he seek the national Conservative leadership that Brian Mulroney ultimately won. Instead, on Thanksgiving weekend 1984 Davis shocked even his closest supporters by announcing his retirement. The Tories seemed set once again to repeat their miraculous cycle of internal rebirth.

Except, for once, that wasn't how it turned out. With victory at the polls seemingly perpetually guaranteed, the Ontario Progressive

Conservative Party was beginning to suffer some of the afflictions reminiscent of a late-Soviet-era regime: the party was arrogant, out of touch, and riven with internal factions. Its right wing in particular agitated against Davis's penchant for state enterprises—a public television network, an oil company—and his decision, without consultation, to extend full funding to grade 13 for Roman Catholic schools. The right succeeded in vaulting Provincial Treasurer Frank Miller, a Muskoka car dealer who promised to emphasize the noun in his party's name over its adjective, into the leadership over progressives Larry Grossman and Dennis Timbrell. Meanwhile, the Liberals had hired an image-maker to spruce up their new leader, David Peterson, a good-looking and smooth-talking London businessman, while the NDP had the youthful, intellectually gifted, and telegenic Bob Rae, who had taken over the leadership in 1982. Suddenly Miller and his Conservatives seemed very old, not helped by the leader's faint Muskoka twang and fondness for plaid jackets. In the provincial election campaign of May 1985, the media, bored with the same old Conservatives, hounded the Tory leader, accusing him of campaigning within a cocoon while being devoid of new ideas. The Liberals, in contrast, were promising everything from an end to extra billing by medical practitioners to allowing beer and wine to be sold in corner stores—the most unkept promise in Ontario politics. On election night, although the vote splits worked in the Tories' favour, giving the Progressive Conservatives 52 seats to the Liberals' 48 and the NDP's 25, the Liberals actually surpassed the Conservatives in the popular vote (37.9% to 37%). The Conservatives had managed with minorities before, but this time the smell of death was in the air.

Rae offered Peterson a deal that would allow the second-place Liberals to become the government. In exchange for implementing a jointly negotiated accord of social action—which included a ban on extra billing; extending rent control; affirmative action for women, minorities, and the handicapped; increased social housing;

tougher environmental laws; more subsidized daycare; and pro-union labour legislation—the NDP would support a Liberal government in the legislature for two years. The Liberals happily signed the accord, for they were predisposed to much of its agenda already.

After a decade of recession and "stagflation"—the miserable combination of high inflation and no growth that afflicted Canada and the West in the early 1980s—Ontario's economy had finally started to expand again, fuelled by falling oil prices, a weaker Canadian dollar that made industry more internationally competitive, and a booming American market. With half of all immigrants flooding into urban southern Ontario, its industries booming, and its cities swelling, now was the time for government action on the social front. It fit with the image of the new Liberal regime. Peterson was young; he had a beautiful wife, the actress Shelley Peterson; he had run an electronics business, which sounded high tech; and he dressed with casual effectiveness—white shirt, the sleeves rolled up, and a trademark loosened Liberal red tie. Although he had first appeared on the scene in 1982 sporting a five-o'clock shadow, thick plastic glasses, and bangs, an image-maker had done wonders in transforming the leader into a deliberately more tousled and populist personality. Peterson radiated youth, action, social conscience, enthusiasm. Astonishing provincial growth of 5.3 per cent in real terms in 1985, 6.1 per cent in 1986, 4.5 per cent in 1987, and an amazing 6.7 per cent in 1988 provided virtually full employment, higher incomes, and a frenzied real estate boom, especially in Toronto. Tax revenues from growth, coupled with increases in sales and income taxes that few, as yet, seemed to mind, allowed the Liberals to fulfil most of their contractual obligations easily. A fresh election in 1987 secured Peterson an astounding majority, with 95 of 130 seats going his way.

It was a halcyon summer, hot and sunny, with the blow-dried premier sauntering across the province flipping hamburgers at Liberal Party picnics and promising that the febrile good times that

George Brown. The founding father of Ontario eventually succumbed to a vision of Canada that would have rendered its largest province a glorified municipality.

Sir John A. Macdonald, first father of Confederation. He dreamed of an all-powerful central government, but Ontario Premier Oliver Mowat, his arch enemy, defeated him at every turn.

Sir Oliver Mowat. Macdonald called him "the little tyrant," because he fought long, hard, and triumphantly against Macdonald to preserve Ontario rights.

The Interprovincial Conference at Quebec City, 1887. Macdonald ignored the rebellious meeting of provincial leaders, a precedent carried through by prime ministers to this day.

Edward Blake, first premier of Ontario, and the first to insist that the federal government keep out of areas of provincial jurisdiction.

Sir Robert Borden. He led Canada though the Great War, vastly increased its fiscal powers, and gave us the income tax.

The Dominion-Provincial Conference of 1927, Prime Minister William Lyon Mackenzie King (centre), with premiers Howard Ferguson of Ontario (left) and L.P. Taschereau of Quebec (right). Taschereau and Ferguson fought for the rights of the provinces to generate hydro-electric power anywhere within their borders, without federal interference.

King and Ontario Premier Mitch Hepburn during the good times, 1934. Hepburn at first worshipped King, but eventually came to hate him so fiercely that his loathing could only have been the product of a diseased mind.

Ontario Premier George Drew (centre). The "twenty-two points" he scrawled on the back of an envelope would guide Progressive Conservatives in Ontario for the next forty-two years.

Ontario Premier Leslie Frost (left) and Toronto Mayor Allen Lamport officially open the Toronto subway, March 1954. Frost virtually created modern industrial Ontario, but at the price of sacrificing the province's autonomy to the federal government.

Ontario Premier John Robarts is serenaded by musicians in this 1968 photo. Notwithstanding such political theatre, Robarts considered himself the quintessential "management man." "This is the era of the management man," he once said.

Ontario Premier Bill Davis pays a courtesy call on Prime Minister Pierre Elliott Trudeau, March 1971. When all others turned against him, Davis would remain the prime minister's staunchest ally. And why not? There was cheap oil in it for Ontario.

Pierre Trudeau during the Trudeaumania days. By the end of his tenure, in 1984, Canada would have a new constitution, and most regions of the country would be estranged from the federal government.

Left to right: Conservative leader Mike Harris, NDP leader Bob Rae, and Liberal Premier David Peterson mug for the cameras before the leaders' debate, August 1990. Rae and Peterson formed a pact in 1985 that let the Liberals govern with NDP support for two years. The pact made Peterson temporarily popular, but he eventually lost power to Rae in 1990, who inherited their accord's fiscally disastrous policies.

Ontario Premier Mike Harris, Alberta Premier Ralph Klein, and Quebec Premier Lucien Bouchard, at the Premiers Conference in Jasper, Alberta, August 1996. The resulting Calgary Accord by the English-speaking premiers would assert that no province could be granted a power not shared by all.

Canadian Alliance Leader Stockwell Day. He lost the 2000 election, but his party embodies beliefs that, if enacted, would fundamentally reshape the federation, stripping Ottawa of many of its powers.

had followed so many bleak years would last forever. "He was pretty, his wife was pretty, his kids were pretty, his dog even,"[2] a bemused ad expert marvelled. One reporter described the campaign as "the Second Coming. There would be a flood of people following him, trying to touch the border of his Roots sweatshirt. Liberals would hold up babies for him to kiss."[3] In those months, David Peterson may have been the most popular premier Ontario had ever seen. He was the leader of a province of funky new downtown restaurant strips—Queen Street West, Elgin Street, Hess Village—of twentysomething stockbrokers in love with Lamborghinis and cocaine, of the $350,000 starter home in Lawrence Park, of the latest all-glass office tower.

Three years later, the provincial economy and Peterson's political career would lie in ruins. The Liberals had themselves and the federal government to blame.

No sooner had Peterson won his first majority government than the wheels began to wobble. Fundamentally, his regime was at odds with governments across the English-speaking world. Regardless of their actual practice, other administrations were at least preaching from the same bible of fiscal restraint, of reassessing expensive social safety nets and questioning the value of centrally managed economies. The Western world had just struggled through more than a decade of weak growth, recessions, and deficits. In Great Britain, Margaret Thatcher had launched the neo-conservative revolution of privatization and tax-and-spending cuts that would transform Britain's moribund economy. In the United States, Ronald Reagan was preaching (though by no means practising) the mantra of deficit containment through spending cuts. In Canada, the Conservative regime of Brian Mulroney worried about the chronic federal deficits and the dangerous imbalance between Canadian and American levels of taxation. But in Ontario it was still 1965. Even the glory days of the great postwar boom couldn't match the expansion of the state that David Peterson presided over. Spending by the Ontario government under the Liberals increased 70 per cent in five years, from $26.4 billion to $45 billion. Spending on health increased from $8.3 billion to $13.6 billion, on social services from $2.6 billion to $5 billion, on education from $3.2 billion to $5 billion. Yet, despite this massive bloating of the Ontario government, the Peterson regime actually balanced the budget in 1989–90, thanks in part to revenue from the economic boom, in part to an unanticipated increase in federal transfers (the product of arcane accounting practices), and in part to an audacious program of new and increased taxes. Provincial income taxes under the Liberals increased from 48 per cent of the federal tax to 53 per cent (not to mention the surtaxes on upper incomes),* and the sales tax increased from 7 per cent to 8 per cent. Treasurer Robert Nixon also hiked or introduced taxes on land transfers, gasoline, alcohol, cigarettes, and anything else he could think of, even tires. This combination of high spending and high taxes would leave the province cruelly exposed when revenues crashed at the onset of the Great Recession of 1990–91.

Ontario's largesse had an immediate and unpleasant impact on the rest of the country as well. The western provinces had been hit hard by falling energy, lumber, and mineral prices. Lacking Ontario's robust manufacturing and service sectors, they struggled with high unemployment and low growth. Quebec, buoyed by the same economic stimulants that superheated the Ontario economy, did somewhat better, but the Atlantic provinces remained chronically weak. Under the circumstances, most of the country needed economic stimulation, especially through lower interest rates. But

* Provincial income tax has traditionally been assessed as a percentage of federal tax. If Ottawa taxes you one dollar, Ontario taxes you 53 cents. Surtaxes are taxes imposed on top of other taxes.

the Bank of Canada was determined to keep inflation in check, and growth in Ontario was pushing the national inflation rate steadily higher, from 4 per cent in 1985 to 5.8 per cent in 1989. To contain the Ontario-induced inflation, the Bank of Canada raised interest rates, to 9.7 per cent in 1988, 12.3 per cent in 1989, and 13 per cent in 1990, a price the rest of the country had to pay. Grant Devine of Saskatchewan bitterly observed that his province's farmers had been flung into the front lines of a war against inflation for which Ontario was to blame.

As interest rates climbed, so did the value of the dollar—thereby weakening export competitiveness and jeopardizing the economic growth on which the expansion depended. In response, the Ontario Liberals did even more harm. The Mulroney government was determined to bring the federal deficit under control, while reducing income taxes to make Canadian industry more competitive. But when Finance Minister Michael Wilson simplified and lowered taxes in 1988, Ontario vitiated this effect by raising its own personal income tax rates. As if that weren't enough, the Peterson government decided in 1989 to provide huge increases in welfare payments, to lessen the gap between rich and poor. Since the federal government was committed to paying 50 per cent of provincial welfare costs, it faced being dragged along. Ottawa retaliated in 1989 by imposing a 5 per cent ceiling on increases to the Canada Assistance Plan for the "have" provinces of Ontario, British Columbia, and Alberta. (Once again, other provinces had to pay for Ontario's actions.) Peterson's successor would be faced with dire consequences of the "cap on CAP," as welfare caseloads mushroomed.

For almost forty years, the Ontario and federal governments had cooperated, with Ottawa taking careful account of Ontario's needs before embarking on policies that might inhibit its wealth-generating capacity. In exchange, successive Ontario governments supported federal government policies. The Pearson and Trudeau administrations existed in large measure because Ontario voters created them.

In virtually every election after the Second World War—the exceptions were the minority governments of Diefenbaker in 1962 and Trudeau in 1972—the party that won the majority of seats in Ontario also won the election. Since the regimes in both Ottawa and Toronto existed at the sufferance of the same voter, it behooved them to get along. The 1984 federal election and 1985 Ontario election changed all that. Peterson had no time for Mulroney's self-proclaimed parsimony; the Ontario Liberals were wedded to a policy of state expansion, not neo-conservative cost-cutting. Mulroney, for his part, was much less wedded to the needs of Ontario than were his predecessors. His government was strong in every region; 32 per cent of its seats came from Ontario, 27 per cent from the West, and 27 per cent from Quebec.

In fact, there was much about the Mulroney regime's feudal coalition of regional fiefdoms that was fundamentally antagonistic towards Ontario. Mulroney depended for his support on soft nationalists in Quebec anxious to wrest a better deal from the rest of Canada, and western conservatives still furious at Ontario and the Liberals for robbing them of their oil revenues. At its heart, the Mulroney coalition was either indifferent or actively hostile to Ontario's interests, a coalition whose resentments only increased in the wake of the Ontario government's disregard for the consequences of its economic actions on other parts of the country.

Even personality was involved. Mulroney was an Anglo-Irish Quebecer, full of the bonhomie, blarney, and street smarts that took him to the upper rungs of the Quebec corporate ladder. He repulsed many central Canadian liberals, who abhorred his policy of cuts to national institutions such as VIA Rail and the CBC, and who dubbed him "Lyin' Brian" over his relaxed approach to conflict-of-interest allegations against members of his cabinet. At a personal as well as a political level, Mulroney and Ontario just didn't get along.

At times it seemed that the federal government was out to get the province. In 1986 Ottawa announced its intentions to designate

Montreal and Vancouver, but not Toronto, as international financial centres, with concomitant tax breaks. Despite protests from Queen's Park, the feds went ahead with the designation in 1987. It turned out to mean little, but the symbolism was galling to Ontario. Mulroney also set out to negotiate energy agreements with the West and with Newfoundland and Nova Scotia. The final accords gave the Atlantic provinces substantial control over the development of and revenues from offshore oil, while going a long way to ensure that nothing like the National Energy Program would ever be foisted on the West again. The deals with the regions signalled Ottawa's intent to protect their interests, even if they impinged on the interests of Ontario.

In one of his sporadic efforts to make peace with the provinces, Trudeau in 1977 had handed "tax points"—a portion of Ottawa's taxing authority—back to the provincial governments, while rolling targeted grants for health care and education into a single block grant. Then, in the first instance of what was to become a chronic federal-provincial sore spot, the Liberals began cutting back the grants. Established Program Financing, as it was called, declined slowly but steadily through the 1980s. The cuts had no singular effect on Ontario—all provinces suffered equally under the per capita federal reductions—but they exacerbated the increasing tension between Queen's Park and Parliament Hill. The feds were pushing Ontario out of their camp as a loyal ally and into the camp of the other resentful provinces—except that Ontario wasn't just another province. It was the one that mattered. If Manitoba is unhappy, Manitoba is unhappy. If Ontario is unhappy, everyone is miserable.

For more than a hundred years, from the National Policy to the National Energy Program, the federal and Ontario governments had agreed that the fundamental economic strategy of Canada must be to preserve Ontario's industrial strength by promoting east-west trade through a common economic union, buttressed by high tariffs to discourage imports. The policy had worked for Ontario, producing a healthy balance of national and international trade. As late as 1980 a larger portion of Ontario's gross domestic product consisted of trade with the rest of Canada than with the United States ($36 billion to $28 billion). But an increasing number of business and government leaders were convinced that Macdonald's old National Policy had outlived its time and that Canada must change its trade policy or risk stagnation. A royal commission launched by Trudeau and charged with strengthening Canada's economic union betrayed its mandate when former Liberal finance minister Donald Macdonald argued, instead, that Canada must drop its tariffs and enter into free trade with the United States. And that deal needed to be reached sooner rather than later: American anger over the investment restrictions of the Foreign Investment Review Agency and the attempt to reverse American domination of the oil sector through the National Energy Program made Canada vulnerable to the threat of trade protectionism in the United States. If the Americans threw up high tariffs against imports of Canadian oil and gas, lumber and minerals, or even—Lord spare us—the auto sector, Canada would be left to trade with nothing but itself, a population smaller than Poland's spread across an expanse that rivals Russia's. If tariffs went down, however, the vast American market would be open to Canadian manufacturers, retailers, and financial institutions. Philosophically attracted to his Republican American cousin, Ronald Reagan, pressured by business groups such as the Canadian Manufacturers' Association, and assured of support by his allied governments in Quebec and western Canada—both of which wanted to escape dependence on Ontario and to forge independent relationships with the United States—Mulroney repudiated his earlier stand against free trade and launched negotiations with the American government, to David Peterson's great distress.

In some ways, the free trade debate left Peterson in a cleft stick. As a businessman, he appreciated the argument against tariffs.

Ontario had prospered as much from the Auto Pact—a quasi–free trade agreement—as it had from the economic union. And Ontario's own business community was agitating for an end to tariffs and a crack at the American market. But as the debate progressed, the Ontario premier moved steadily from a position of strong reservation to outright opposition to free trade, making him the sole and improbable ally of Joe Ghiz, premier of Prince Edward Island, in provincial opposition to the deal.

In part, Peterson's opposition was historical: the old National Policy had served Ontario well for more than a century, so what need was there to change it? In part it was contemporary: the Ontario economy was booming, so why risk the current prosperity on such an enormous economic gamble? In part it was idealistic: the deal was fiercely opposed by the labour movement and by intellectual and cultural elites of the province as a betrayal of the nation. The imperialist Americans who, they lamented, already dominated our culture and economy, would suppress it completely once the last barrier was lowered, so opposition made Peterson appear civilized and enlightened. And in part it was pragmatic: the underdeveloped economies of the other regions gambled little when they gambled with free trade, since trade in natural resources, on which their economies were based, was almost exclusively one way in their favour. It would be another thing, however, to throw the steel mills of Hamilton, the banks of Toronto, and the burgeoning high-technology centre of Ottawa-Carleton up against their American counterparts. Granted, the gains might ultimately outweigh the losses—and most business leaders appeared ready to take the risk—but the losses, especially in the short term, would be enormous. Ontario industry was obsolescent, compared with its American counterparts, and its wages and benefits were uncompetitively high. Tariffs were all that kept the American branch plants, which were such an integral part of Ontario's manufacturing sector, alive. Why keep a Westinghouse plant open in Ontario when, without tariffs, an American plant could service the Canadian market without so much as a retool? So, fighting the free trade deal made Peterson a conservative.

Ontario had in some measure brought the misfortune of free trade on itself, by demanding the National Energy Program that angered the Americans and raising the threat of the very sanctions that the free trade deal was intended to prevent. Moreover, free trade would circumscribe the ability of an Ottawa–Queen's Park alliance to impose any future NEP-style programs on the West. As Thomas Courchene has noted, "From the western perspective, the energy components of the FTA [Free Trade Agreement] were every bit as much about containing Ontario hegemony as they were about energy continentalism."[4]

But what mattered most was that the alliance between the Ontario and federal governments had been shattered. Far from tailoring its economic policies primarily to the perceived needs of Ontario, Ottawa had embarked on a policy that, to many eyes, gave advantage to the rest of the country at Ontario's expense. To protest the betrayal, Peterson campaigned against Mulroney during the 1988 federal election, though not with the fervour of a partisan politician determined to bring down a mortal enemy. The Ontario premier was too nervous about further alienating an already estranged business community. And free trade was a winning issue for Mulroney in 1988, helping him secure a second majority government; it hardly profited Peterson to ally himself with the losing cause of the federal Liberal Party. But the Free Trade Agreement that was finally signed in both countries in 1988 represented more than the end of the National Policy and a huge gamble, with the future of Ontario's industrial heartland at stake. It represented the end of an economic alliance that had served the interests of both Parliament Hill and Queen's Park for almost forty years. That alliance would never be reforged. From that date on, Ontario was just another alienated province. As historian H.V. Nelles said, it would lead Ontario to "shed its mantle of statesmanship and renew instead its historical role as the spoilt child of Confederation."[5]

The rupture was not yet complete, however. On the constitutional front, Ontario remained ready, aye, ready to support the federal government in its efforts to cement the federation. Indeed, David Peterson became obsessed with constitutional reform, staking his political career on it—a gamble he lost. Brian Mulroney was determined to make Quebec a willing signatory to the constitution. When Robert Bourassa, as close to being a federalist as Quebec was ever likely to get, returned to power in 1985, the door seemed open for a deal. It helped that Peterson, Ontario's first bilingual premier, and Bourassa had liked each other from the moment they met at a Liberal convention back in 1977. Peterson saw Ontario's role in the negotiations as the helpful fixer, willing to act as a bridge between federal and provincial interests, interpreter of Quebec to the rest of Confederation. While in the old days Ontario premiers had ganged up with Quebec premiers to combat the federal interest, Peterson saw Ontario as one member of a tripartite alliance with the federal and Quebec governments. Together, they would persuade the rest of the country to accede to a new constitutional arrangement that would bring Quebec back into the fold.

Peterson enthusiastically participated in the agreement, signed by the eleven first ministers at Meech Lake in Gatineau Park in June 1987, that recognized Quebec as a "distinct society" and offered a limited expansion of the powers and rights of all provinces. He went further, extending services for francophones in Ontario, including the creation of the province's first French-language school board in Ottawa-Carleton and the first French-language community college. But when Bourassa used the existing constitution's notwithstanding clause to override a Supreme Court ruling that struck down the Quebec law mandating French as the language on commercial signs, the Ontario premier suffered the consequence. Seventy municipalities across Ontario reacted with anglophone intransigence by designating themselves "English only," whatever that meant. Peterson further alienated himself from his own constituency by giving away a parcel of Ontario seats in the Senate in a last-minute bid to salvage the deal during marathon negotiations in June 1990. It was for naught: Elijah Harper, representing the First Nations, held up ratification in the Manitoba legislature until after the June 23 deadline had passed, while Clyde Wells in Newfoundland refused to bring it before his legislature for a vote. The Meech Lake accord was dead, and the smell of its carcass clung to its champions, including Brian Mulroney in Ottawa and David Peterson in Toronto.

It will forever be a matter of speculation just how much the contamination of Meech's failure contributed to Peterson's defeat in the election he called a few weeks after it died. Resentment over the opportunism of calling the election only three years into his mandate, a worsening economic climate, petty scandals, and constant protests from the environmentalists, teachers, and public servants who should have been the government's staunchest allies probably had, collectively, more to do with it. "In this business, there are some things you die for," Peterson responded, when a cabinet minister warned him that his obsession with Meech was "going to kill us, politically."[6] As it was, he died without a friend, for the federation he had fought so hard to renew through Meech Lake had already united to betray Ontario through free trade. The final irony would be that free trade freed Ontario from the rest of the country far more than it freed the rest of the country from Ontario. But that is a later story.

First, Ontario had to endure the consequences of the past fifteen years of Liberal and Conservative interventionist government: of creeping state expansion, steadily rising taxes, obsolescent industries exploiting cheap energy and a low dollar to avoid competing openly on the international market, an obsession with constitutional process over economic substance, and the dangerous divorce of interests between the federal and Ontario governments. The piper had arrived, demanding payment for all his tunes. The Great Recession was here.

Bob Rae never thought he would be premier of Ontario. The New Democratic Party he led had offered no coherent and attractive alternative to the policies of David Peterson during the three years of his majority government. Rae himself was pessimistic about his chances in the 1990 campaign, hoping for no better than 30 per cent of the popular vote—which would be a signal success for the New Democratic Party—and confiding to his wife, Arlene Perly Rae, that, regardless of the result, he planned to step down after the election. That promise, of course, did not envision the prospect that he would actually become premier.

The socialists had come close once. In 1943, under the leadership of Ted Jolliffe—a Rhodes scholar, just like Rae—the Co-operative Commonwealth Federation came within four seats of forming a minority government. Instead, the Progressive Conservatives of George Drew took the reins, ending nine years of Hepburn Liberalism, and, with Drew's "twenty-two points" in hand, proceeded to govern for the next forty-two years. In 1975 the oratorically brilliant Stephen Lewis had pushed the party into second-place status during the first minority government of Bill Davis, but although Lewis was much beloved of the Toronto intellectual mafia, he came across to many people, in the words of one journalist, as "an arrogant, ruthless fanatic who would have the whole province eating sugar cane given half a chance."[7] The NDP were never really a credible alternative government to the Conservatives during Davis's tenure, any more than they were to the Conservatives or Liberals in 1985. Many Dippers blamed Rae for signing an accord with the Liberals that year that tacitly made the NDP a junior partner in a coalition, without even the advantage of seats in cabinet. But Rae was simply acknowledging the reality of the impossibility of an NDP victory at the polls; instead, as the party always has during minority governments, it was exploiting its kingmaker status to advance its social agenda. No one, not least the NDP, expected anything to change when, in July 1990, Peterson called for a fresh mandate after only three years of majority government.

But no one, not even the pollsters, had anticipated the deepening disenchantment of the Ontario electorate. This disenchantment was, itself, unprecedented. The Ontario political culture, after all, was perhaps the most historically stable in the Western world, a fruitful amalgam of pro-British, traditional Tory values and the liberal democratic spirit of Reform—its founding conservative and progressive impulses. The Tories had crushed the Reformers in the Rebellion of 1837; the Reformers had gradually usurped the powers of the Tories in the years that followed. Oliver Mowat had employed his political genius to merge both strands into an institutional political culture that celebrated the British conservative tradition along with the egalitarian and socially progressive impulses of reform. "Do not be carried away by names, my dear fellow," he advised an associate, when explaining his decision to stand as a Liberal. "One party has sometimes had most virtue on its side, and the other party has had it at other times."[8] Mowat had demonstrated the enormous political appeal to Ontarians of moderately progressive social policies cloaked in conservative ethos—progressive conservatism, in other words. That, and a strong dose of Ontario nationalism, secured him twenty-four years as premier of Ontario. Mitch Hepburn, though more turbulent than his predecessors, as the times of Depression and war dictated, adjusted the mix, supporting progressive sentiments while governing like a reactionary conservative. Finally, the Progressive Conservative Party successfully exploited Mowat's formula after the Second World War for forty-two years. The lesson seemed clear: Ontario voters prized a cautious blend of liberal policies constrained by fiscal pragmatism, and stability above all. When David Peterson finally ended four decades of Progressive Conservative rule, many political observers assumed that the mantle had been transferred, at least until the shattered Progressive Conservatives rebuilt their party sufficiently to mount a comeback.

But with the self-satisfaction of hindsight, we can detect fault lines that were threatening to undermine Ontario's fabled political stability. Massive immigration after the Second World War from Europe and Asia had at least partially submerged the province's Anglo-American historical roots. Western societies everywhere were experiencing what came to be called "the decline of deference," as volatile voters abandoned their ancestors' stable voting habits and shopped for political parties that best seemed to satisfy their demands. Most important, perhaps, Peterson had dangerously tampered with the progressive-conservative formula, emphasizing social spending at the expense of moderation and fiscal prudence. The price was about to be paid. Ontario's economy, while apparently booming, had for a decade and a half been pushing itself ever closer to a precipice from which there was less and less chance of escape. The combination of subsidized energy and higher wages engineered in the 1970s made the province singularly vulnerable to competition, once energy prices began to decline in the 1980s. The consequences of that decline were initially delayed, when a falling Canadian dollar masked the inherent uncompetitiveness of Ontario's goods and services. But by 1990 an entire bevy of chickens was coming home to roost. Energy prices were reaching record lows. The Free Trade Agreement that came into effect on January 1, 1989, exposed Ontario's industries to the full force of American competition, while stripping them of their captive Canadian market. And the inflationary taxation and spending policies of the Peterson regime had forced the Bank of Canada to raise interest rates, strangling investment and driving up the value of the Canadian dollar—all of which further weakened Ontario's competitive advantage. To top it off, the international economy decided it was time for another recession.

Ontario voters were only dimly aware of the gathering economic storm. True, unemployment appeared to be on the rise, but only the Liberals knew of the urgent warnings coming from the bureaucrats at the Ministry of Finance: revenues were dropping dramatically, and the forecasted $30 million surplus for that year's budget was about to turn into a $3 billion deficit. But if the public was still unaware of the problems with the books, they were very aware of, and increasingly unhappy with, Peterson's obsession with constitutional issues, the high taxes he had imposed, the government's vulnerability to the persistent demands of social, environmental, and labour groups who never seemed content, and the political opportunism of the early election call. Unsettled, annoyed, worried, they cast about for an alternative.

The Progressive Conservatives were in no shape to govern anything, including themselves. Since their defeat in 1985 the party had descended into chaos and debt, emerging mere weeks before the election with a new leader, an unknown backbencher from North Bay called Mike Harris. His simplistic message—cut taxes, cut taxes, cut taxes—hardly seemed a credible recipe for a major modern economy faced with a host of structural challenges. "A right-wing dinosaur," his critics dubbed him, whose "extreme views and his astonishing vacillations on vital policy areas were widely documented."[9] Besides, he was a Conservative. Brian Mulroney, whose Goods and Services Tax and failure over Meech Lake had helped make him perhaps the least popular prime minister in Canadian history, was also a Conservative. It was just a bad time for Conservatives.

That left Bob Rae.

There he stood, neatly tailored in one of four very respectable suits he had purchased at Harry Rosen's for the campaign, his attractive and intelligent wife by his side, chipping away at the Liberals over their record of scandal, their arrogance, their detachment from ordinary people. “The strategy,” a campaign insider later confided, “was really simple. Peterson doesn’t listen to you, he listens to a select group of powerful people who can rent space in his ear. He doesn’t listen to you and the NDP will listen to you.”[10] One proposed NDP ad, which the squeamish leadership finally vetoed, had the sounds of bedsprings creaking while the voiceover asked, “Who’s in bed with the Liberals now?” The only problem was that, when voters and reporters finally turned to the socialists in the middle of the election campaign and asked them what they would do if elected, the party had few answers. Realizing their plight, a small team of advisers frantically cranked out a platform over three days, promising everything from public auto insurance to 10,000 new childcare spaces a year. The financial assumptions behind the platform did not bear close scrutiny, so the party released it to the public the day before the leaders’ debate. They correctly reckoned it would be swept aside by the theatrics of the televised contest.

Still, even though polls began showing a marked swing away from the Liberals and towards the NDP in the last half of the campaign, no one, including the NDP, thought it could actually win. “I never believed that we would form the government, even during the last week of the campaign,” Rae later confessed. “I really didn’t.”[11] And it was a close-run thing: on election night, the NDP secured only 37.6 per cent of the vote, normally not enough for a majority government. But the miracle of three-party vote splits this time worked in the NDP’s favour, securing them 74 of 130 seats, a solid majority. With fine historical irony, the greatest surge for the party came in southwestern Ontario, ancient home of radical reform. David Peterson was defeated in his own London riding and resigned as leader on the very night of the election. Whether or not they intended it, the voters had sent Bob Rae to the premier’s office.

And, in truth, there was justice in the decision. For the past five years, Ontario had been governed by a set of policies and principles jointly crafted in 1985 by the Liberals and the New Democrats. For these five years the Liberals had been charged with implementing the program. For the next five years the NDP would bear the responsibility of dealing with its consequences—the only difference being that the Liberals governed during times of apparent prosperity, while the NDP would be cursed with a recession second only in its severity to the Great Depression itself.

The Rae government was confronted with two acute crises immediately it took office. First, the province was heading into recession. According to the alarming statistics being gathered at the Ministry of Finance, the economy was expected to shrink by more than 3 per cent in 1991. Unemployment was skyrocketing, and would ultimately vault from 5 to 10 per cent. Unlike traditional economic downturns, in which Canada enters into the recession after the United States, and Ontario after the rest of Canada, Ontario appeared to be leading the continent in the rush to the bottom, thanks to its unique combination of high taxes and interest rates, uncompetitive industries, and the sudden shock of free trade. The Rae government had two choices: curtail spending in an effort to prevent the budget from going seriously out of balance, or maintain or even increase spending in hopes of counteracting the recession's effects on the economy. This decision, one that would define the government, should have consumed all the new premier's energies and attention. But there was another, equally compelling, crisis on the constitution front. Neither issue could be put off.

Robert Bourassa and most Quebecers were infuriated by the rejection of the Meech Lake accord and the distinct society status it would have conferred on Quebec. Now even federalist Quebecers were warning that the province might have no choice but to abandon Confederation. Bourassa gave Mulroney two years to come up with a proposal that would satisfy the aspirations of Quebec.

Otherwise, he couldn't say what would happen. In the meantime, there would be no further discussions about the constitution with the other provinces.

Bob Rae, in his heart, may always have been more of a federal than a provincial politician. Unlike most Ontario premiers, who hailed from small towns or small cities, Rae was raised in Ottawa, the son of an influential diplomat, got his political start in the House of Commons, and came only reluctantly to the provincial leadership of his party. Whatever economic crisis might be taking shape in the near distance, Rae temperamentally was drawn to the question of nation-building, or at least nation-preserving. Within months of his election he was consulting with Bourassa in Florida. From there it was inevitable that he would soon be rocking on the front porch of Mulroney's Harrington Lake retreat, listening to the aggrieved prime minister recalling lost battles. "Clyde sat as close to me as you are now, Bob, and told me to my face that he would have a vote. And now he's the darling of the media ... Why? When he has broken his word?"[12]

Rae had several points to make at the rocking-chair summit that were unusual for a postwar Ontario premier. First, the province would not sit by and let the federal government negotiate a new deal on behalf of the rest of the country with Quebec. This was a surprise. Ever since the entente between Leslie Frost and Louis St. Laurent, Ontario had served in the shadow of the federal government in constitutional affairs. There were exceptions, of course—John Robarts' Confederation of Tomorrow Conference was an explicit attempt at advancing constitutional reform through an Ontario-driven provincial conference—but, increasingly over time, Ontario had cleaved to the federal interest, helpfully asking what it might do, what Senate seats it might give up, to assist the cause. Now the cause was almost lost and Bourassa was tossing around ultimatums, one of which was that Quebec was interested only in bilateral negotiations with the federal government. Ten years earlier,

Queen's Park might have placed its trust in Ottawa to negotiate on its behalf. No more. Jeff Rose, a former labour negotiator whom Rae had brought in as deputy minister of intergovernmental affairs (with Rae himself taking the portfolio), would soon be in contact with his English Canadian provincial counterparts, rallying them to unite in demanding that any new negotiations towards a constitution involve all the provinces. And Ontario had several unique demands of its own: the provinces must assent to any proposal to Quebec, and Aboriginal leaders must also be included in the negotiations. Further, Rae wanted a social charter incorporated into the new constitution, one that would enshrine in law the obligation of the federal and provincial governments to the social safety net that New Democrats had helped to create.

Most important for Rae was that Mulroney should understand that Ontario was changing. It no longer saw itself as the loyal lieutenant of Ottawa. The federal government had reneged on its side of the deal by supporting free trade, cutting transfer payments, and signing energy accords with Atlantic Canada and the West. Confederation no longer favoured Ontario, and Ontario, in response, was turning into just another disgruntled province. Indeed, by leading the provincial charge against a bilateral Ottawa-Quebec accord, it was beginning to revert to its Mowat-era role as a prime antagonist to the federal power.

This was a new role, at least in recent history, for an Ontario premier to play. But Bob Rae was not alone. Within Ontario's universities, political scientists were adding up the pluses and minuses of the province's recent dealings with the rest of Canada and coming to some alarming conclusions. Thomas Courchene, a political economist at Queen's University in Kingston, was a rare example of an academic who sided with the provinces. In 1988 he had delivered a highly controversial series of lectures at York University entitled "What Does Ontario Want?" Courchene looked at Quebec's nationalist, state-driven economic expansion, and the sense of confidence—not to say arrogance—it had engendered in the province, and compared it with Ontario's more troubled relations within the Canadian cartel. The current situation, he maintained, was not to Ontario's advantage. For the sake of a federal union that protected Ontario's access to domestic markets, the province had agreed to let Quebec opt out of social programs that Ontario had preserved for the rest of the country by opting in. It had agreed, as an act of *lèse majesté*, to have substantial amounts of its wealth transferred to poorer regions through equalization payments, although this "generosity" might also have been a ploy to generate sufficient buying power in those regions for them to acquire Ontario goods.

All of this had worked splendidly, Courchene argued, until the upheavals of the 1970s and 1980s shook Ontario's complacent hold on the national agenda. In response, Ontario had launched its own Quiet Revolution. While Quebec had emerged as an increasingly self-confident and self-contained society, and the western provinces were realigning their interests in the wake of the disastrous NEP, "Ontarians emerged from this process more confused about who they are and more divided in terms of what they want."[13] The response was to launch a self-defining social agenda, even as the federal government, Quebec, and other provinces focused on the economic agenda, culminating in free trade. As Ontario's sense of estrangement grew, the province further expanded its taxation and spending policies at the expense of Ottawa's attempts at fiscal control. Alienated from a federal government more concerned with the regions, its policies and priorities contradictory to the rest of Canada, Ontario no longer saw itself as the heartland. "Altruism drives few people and even fewer institutions,"[14] Courchene reminded his listeners. "If the federation comes to be perceived by Ontarians as not adequately reflecting the interests of Ontario, the end result will be a much stronger Queen's Park, a much more decentralized federation and, by definition, a much weaker central government."[15]

Such heresy—an Ontario government acting as a centrifugal rather than centripetal force within Confederation—prompted immediate scorn from some of Courchene's colleagues. "Ontario is too complex a society and there is not enough identity between the population and the provincial government for any sharp ideological choices to be made (at least by Liberal and Conservative governments) which could permanently fly in the face of traditional public attitudes or large sectors of the population," countered Donald Stevenson, who had served as Ontario's deputy minister of intergovernmental affairs. "It is likely, even without a change in government in Ottawa, that the inherent forces working on both the federal and Ontario governments will result, over time, in both governments adopting a closer set of perspectives than they had over the last four years ... [the] isolation of Ontario is unlikely to be a permanent feature."[16]

Others, however, believed that Courchene was right; that, as Professor Nelles of York University put it, "Ontario, by virtue of its economic power and social complexity, is a distinct society too."[17] Most important, Rae believed Courchene. His entire emphasis on attempting to entrench a "social charter" in the Charlottetown accord, he later recalled, was "essential to keeping the national glue in a more devolved Canada."[18] Regardless of the outcome of the constitutional negotiations, Rae was convinced, Canada was headed down a path of decentralization, and the Ontario government was determined to defend its own interests vigorously as the federation devolved. Rae fired this warning shot across the Canadian prime minister's bow at Harrington Lake in 1991, but, although "Mulroney listened ... I don't think he ever saw this as anything more than the predictable chant of a premier."[19]

Mulroney would discover the extent of Ontario's determination in the following months. As specially appointed envoy Joe Clark criss-crossed the country, seeking to broker a deal among the rest of the provinces that could be presented to Quebec, he found Ontario pushing the agenda in a way that Ottawa had no desire to see it go. Ontario insisted that Aboriginals be in on the negotiations; it insisted on a social charter; and, in exchange for accepting a Senate with increased regional representation, it demanded more seats in the House of Commons. The final deal was negotiated among the English Canadian provinces in June 1992 while Mulroney was away in Germany. Ontario agreed to a "Triple-E" Senate—elected, with equal representation by the provinces, and with effective powers—provided those powers were circumscribed and Ontario's influence in the House of Commons was increased. Rae also agreed to have the social charter placed in the preamble of the constitution, where it would not be binding in the courts. In exchange, the other provinces agreed to the inherent right of the First Nations to self-government, and Ontario, playing its ancient role of Quebec's ally, convinced those provinces to give the francophone province a veto on constitutional changes.

The agreement surprised and apparently upset Mulroney, who had assumed that the provinces and Clark would fail to reach consensus, leaving him free to deal with Quebec unilaterally. How he planned to push an Ottawa-Quebec agreement through the provincial parliaments is difficult to fathom. Still, the deal brought Bourassa back to the table and led to yet another round of negotiations. On August 28, 1992, in Charlottetown, the premiers and the prime minister unanimously agreed on a new accord: it recognized Quebec as a distinct society and provided it with a constitutional veto; it delineated the powers of the federal and provincial governments, all to the provinces' advantage; it reformed the Senate; and it provided for Aboriginal self-government. Everyone was happy, except the Canadian population. Overheard cell phone conversations from nationalist Quebec bureaucrats criticizing the deal as a sell-out helped convince Quebecers that the Charlottetown accord was bad for Quebec. The Aboriginal leadership began to partially disavow the deal they had helped negotiate as soon as it became public. Westerners, convinced that political elites had once again sold the country down the river to appease Quebec, were encouraged in their indignation by Preston Manning, leader of the new Reform Party. Feminists, labour leaders, cultural elites, and Trudeauesque nationalists attacked the accord with full force. Many Canadians simply did not trust any deal championed by Lyin' Brian. On October 26, 1992, the night of the referendum, the country voted solidly against the accord. Ontario, Newfoundland, New Brunswick, and Prince Edward Island voted yes, although, in Ontario's case, the result was so razor thin that the spoiled ballets added to the No votes would have constituted a defeat. (The final tally was 49.8 per cent for, 49.6 per cent against, with 0.6 per cent of voters spoiling their ballots.) "The emotional glue holding the country together was becoming unstuck," Rae mournfully concluded.[20] Whether it was or not, the final bond between Ontario and the federal government—the mutual desire to satisfy Quebec's aspirations within a Canadian federation—dissolved that night. With its dissolution, Ontario and Ottawa truly became two solitudes. For on every other front, the two governments were already utterly estranged.

Liberal Treasurer Robert Nixon had forecast a modest $30 million surplus for the budget of fiscal 1990/91. Instead, as Ontario plunged into a terrible recession, revenues collapsed and the budget quickly fell into deficit. Not only was Ontario feeling the effects of the international economic downtown but its manufacturing industries, many of them antiquated and uncompetitive, were facing the full brunt of the Free Trade Agreement. Ontario, which usually suffered less than the rest of Canada during recessions, plunged into a deeper trough than any other province. In industrial Hamilton, steel giants Dofasco and Stelco laid off 45 per cent of their workforce. St. Catharines had a higher unemployment rate than St.

John's, Windsor was hurting worse than Chicoutimi. In Ottawa-Carleton, which had considered itself relatively recession-proof thanks to the federal government and its high-tech industries, public sector downsizing and depressed demand forced almost one-fifth of the population onto unemployment insurance or welfare. The province was in agony.

Ever since the Great Depression of the 1930s, governments had fought recessions by increasing spending to stimulate economic growth. But that response required some combination of higher taxes and budget deficits, and the Peterson regime had hiked income and sales taxes so high that Ontario had moved from one of the lowest-taxed jurisdictions in the country to one of the highest. Even worse, the Liberals had increased benefits for people on welfare, just as the rolls began to swell. The federal government, alarmed at the fiscal implications for its own strained finances if it maintained its agreement to share welfare costs fifty-fifty with a province determined to ratchet up benefits, had imposed the 5 per cent limit on increases to the Canada Assistance Plans, the "cap on CAP." As welfare caseloads burgeoned from 315,000 in 1989 to 395,000 in 1990 and 532,000 in 1991, the Ontario government found itself responsible for almost the entire costs of the increased caseload.

The Rae government had precious little room to manoeuvre as Finance Minister Floyd Laughren approached his first budget in the winter of 1991. The prudent course would have been to preserve what was left of investor confidence and protect the province from escalating debt interest payments by cutting back benefits and other government services. But social democrats do not fight recessions by cutting welfare rates. Social democracy is about government intervention in market forces for the social welfare. Spending commitments would be preserved—in fact, they would be enhanced. The deficit would be allowed to rise to $10 billion. The recession would not last long, went the reasoning, and the books should come into balance in a year or two, once growth resumed. In the meantime, the government would be there for those who needed it. On the afternoon of April 19, 1991, Laughren rose in the Ontario legislature and told the people of Ontario: "We had a choice to make this year—to fight the deficit or fight the recession. We are proud to be fighting the recession."[21]

In retrospect, the 1991 budget was a mortal mistake for the Rae regime and a terrible punishment to inflict on the province. The deficit was not ephemeral: thanks to NDP anti-recession policies, it quickly became entrenched. The government not only maintained Peterson's spending commitments but added the jobsOntario job-creation program as well, diverting from the treasury money that was vitally needed for health, education, law enforcement, and other programs—all to create jobs that disappeared as soon as the government money ran out.

And that was only the beginning. The Liberals had already raised welfare rates; now the NDP decided to raise them again. A worker with children could earn more on welfare than by holding down a minimum-wage job. The combination of federal regulations that pushed people off unemployment insurance more quickly, the deep and entrenched recession, and the generosity of the welfare package sent caseloads into the stratosphere, to 623,000 in 1993. The budget of the Ministry of Community and Social Services nearly doubled between 1990 and 1995, from $5 billion to $9.5 billion.

As if that weren't enough, the Rae government also decided that the public service should be insulated from the hard times. In 1991 the Ontario government allowed public sector salaries to rise by an average 5.8 per cent. This was folly. Not only was the provincial government unable to afford such increases, as its revenues continued to drop from out-of-work taxpayers and failing businesses, but the one group of workers least vulnerable to the effects of the recession were government employees, whose numbers were growing, not shrinking, during the downturn.

Given the job-creation programs, public sector pay increases, and topped-up welfare rates, the Ontario government's finances were in a shambles. It had taken from Confederation to 1990 for the government of Ontario to accumulate a debt of $42 billion. In less than five years, the NDP had more than doubled it to $89 billion. Worst of all, the deficit financing probably prolonged the very recession it aimed to fight. Lack of private sector confidence in the government's finances helped ensure that, long after the rest of the country emerged from the recession of the early 1990s, the Ontario economy continued to suffer.

The NDP leadership eventually realized it had made, to put it gently, a series of policy errors. As Laughren prepared for the 1993–94 budget, ministerial staff warned that, unless the government retrenched, the deficit for the coming year would reach $17 billion. Such numbers alarmed even social democrats. The government concluded that the pay increase to the public service had been a mistake and that it needed to reopen the collective agreements to retrieve some of the money. Rae proposed that the unions representing the public service and the broader public sector collaborate with the government to lower wages temporarily in a "Social Contract," although it bore little resemblance to the libertarian philosophies of John Locke. Labour, however, is not in the habit of voluntarily abandoning collective agreements, and public sector labour leaders were furious that a social democratic government would violate such a sacred principle. Rae's former allies became his worst enemies, as the Canadian Union of Public Employees and the Ontario Public Service Employees Union fought bitterly against concessions. In the end, the government compelled compliance under threat of legislation, forcing workers to take unpaid holidays each year. But the "Rae days," as they were quickly dubbed, simply served to add labour to the expanding camp of enemies of the government. The lawns of Queen's Park were carpeted with union protestors decrying their betrayal.

In retrospect, Rae confessed that his "focus on the Charlottetown Accord, unavoidable as it was, took [him] away from the necessary preparation for what was to come on the Social Contract ... I had used my negotiating resources in the year of Charlottetown [summer of 1991 to the summer of 1992], and just didn't have enough left over for what was to follow."[22] The irony was that although Rae had sacrificed his energies serving the lost constitutional cause, Ottawa and Queen's Park remained implacably opposed on economic and other intergovernmental matters. The Mulroney regime's first assault on the Ontario government, the Canada–United States Free Trade Agreement, was followed up in 1994 with a further insult, the North American Free Trade Agreement, that brought the emerging economy of Mexico into the mix of new competitors for Ontario businesses. If Peterson absconded with Wilson's income tax cut, the Conservative finance minister had his own revenge—the Goods and Services Tax—which, coupled with the provincial sales and income tax hikes, caused a fundamental shift in Ontario taxpayers' spending patterns. Citizens became obsessed with avoiding taxes whenever possible, either legally through tax shelters or illegally through barter and undeclared earnings, further depressing provincial government revenues. The federal determination to fight inflation with high interest rates—which starved industry of investment capital and pushed up the Canadian dollar, making Ontario even more uncompetitive—only made things worse.

When the wily and veteran Quebecer Jean Chrétien obliterated the Conservatives under Mulroney's successor, Kim Campbell, in the 1993 federal election, Rae held hopes for improved relations. The Liberals had taken every seat in Ontario but one. Surely now, Rae was convinced, Ottawa would revive its traditional concern for protecting that province's economy. To press the point, the Ontario premier wrote to all ninety-eight Ontario Liberal MPs, pleading his government's case. The cap on CAP, he told them, was costing the Ontario treasury $1.7 billion a year in foregone transfers from Ottawa. The federal government was spending only 27 per cent of its training budget in Ontario, even though the province accounted for 36 per cent of the country's unemployed. Ontario absorbed 55 per cent of Canada's immigrants, but received only 38 per cent of what Ottawa spent on settlement and training. In total, Ontario was being deprived of $2.7 billion annually in funds it would be entitled to if Ottawa funded on a per capita basis. "Ontarians sent a strong clear message last October 25," Rae admonished the members. "They voted for change in Ottawa. They voted for a change in the way Ontario is treated by the federal government."[23]

They received a change, but only for the worse. Paul Martin, Chrétien's tough-nosed finance minister, was determined to eradicate the federal deficit, which by 1993/94 had reached an appalling $42 billion. In his first budget, released in February 1994, he extended the cap on CAP through to 1997. In his second budget, a year later, he went much farther. The federal government consolidated all transfers into a single payment, the Canada Health and Social Transfer. The CHST lowered the overall level of transfers from the federal government to the provinces, but also entrenched the cap on CAP within the transfers to Ontario, Alberta, and British Columbia.

The Liberal response to Ontario's pleas devastated and enraged the NDP government and its premier. Rae had already begun openly to question the fairness of Ottawa's treatment of its largest and most economically important province. His letter to the Ontario MPs was based on a series of papers the provincial government had commissioned showing that Ontario was contributing vastly more to the federal government than it was receiving in return. Fully 5.5 per cent of Ontario's gross domestic product, or $1,506 for every Ontarian, was diverted to other provinces under the federal government's transfer programs. In the years from the late 1970s to the early 1990s, the federal government had "offloaded" through reduced transfers $10.4 billion dollars of its obligations to Ontario. Ontario contributed 43 per cent of all taxes received by the federal government, but the federal government spent only 28 per cent of its subsidies on industries in the province, and 27 per cent of its expenditure on capital assistance. The federal government devoted $358 million to regional support programs in Atlantic Canada, Quebec, and the West, but only $9 million to regional support for equally depressed Northern Ontario. The federal government was signing defence-procurement contracts that stipulated that production and employment *must* be moved out of Ontario.

Free trade, the cap on CAP, high interest rates, the GST, underfunding, the CHST, the failure of Charlottetown and of Meech—there seemed to be not one good thing to be said for relations between Ontario and the federal government. But most Ontarians, perhaps preoccupied with the string of controversies and disasters emanating from Rae's own administration, seemed unaware. The NDP premier was determined to make them see the light. On May 11, 1994, Rae rose in the Ontario legislature to move a resolution attacking the federal government's discriminatory actions against Ontario. "We insist upon the right of Ontarians to a fair share of federal expenditure, which residents of Ontario do not now receive," the resolution demanded. It called for a new federal-provincial financial agreement that involved "no fiscal offloading to the provinces" and "no discriminatory treatment against Canadians living in Ontario." And, it concluded, "the existing discrimination must stop."[24] The resolution passed 90–2. Its message was quickly dubbed "Fair Share Federalism."

The Rae administration, by almost unanimous consent, was a failed administration. The voters delivered their verdict on June 8, 1995, sending the NDP from first to third place in the legislature, with only 21 per cent of the vote and seventeen seats. To the astonishment of most pundits and the leadership of the Liberal Party, the voters chose Mike Harris, the tax-fighting Progressive Conservative, over Lyn McLeod, the Liberal leader, demonstrating that the traditional complacency of the Ontario electorate truly had been replaced by unpredictable volatility. The new Conservative premier promptly set out to dismantle every aspect of the fiscal and social agenda that Bob Rae and David Peterson had entrenched. Within two years, virtually nothing they had created would be left.

Bob Rae produced more than a legacy of discord and debt. He shattered the Ottawa-Ontario entente that had been in place since the Second World War. Under Rae, the Ontario and federal governments became antagonists, not allies. And, by the late 1980s, some observers began to note that Ontario had migrated from being Ottawa's ally to "just another region." But Ontario never has been just another region. It is the centrepiece of the federation. With Rae's demand for participation in the Charlottetown accord, and then his declaration of estrangement over discriminatory federal funding, Ottawa could no longer count on Ontario as its powerful provincial ally in Ottawa's conception of nation-building.

Harris, Rae's polar-opposite successor, would inherit one vital aspect of his predecessor's world view. He would also agree that Confederation worked against Ontario's interests and demand his own fair share. But unlike Rae, Harris would argue from a position of growing and ever more aggressive strength, strength he would not hesitate to wield.

6

Mowat's Heir

When Mike Harris won the leadership of the Ontario Progressive Conservative Party in 1990, only to be thrown immediately into the election called by David Peterson, some wondered whether this contest would be the last the bankrupt, dispirited, marginalized movement would ever fight. The Conservatives had gone in the space of a few years from the institutional governing party of Ontario to a rural fringe, less credible as an alternative to the governing Liberals even than the NDP. And the new leader seemed tailor-made to lead the party to oblivion. His slouching gait, Northern Ontario drawl, leaden speaking style, and lack of advanced education or social graces made him appear a parliamentary relic, a rural throwback to the days of regional party bosses, a figure already going out of style in the era of Leslie Frost.

Shortly before the September 6 election, the party scraped together enough money for one last poll. The prognosis was grim: with the Tories running a distant third in popularity, many of its seventeen existing seats were in jeopardy. The Conservatives could be reduced to four or six seats. "We actually *owe* votes in Downsview," the pollster joked grimly. David Lindsay, Harris's most senior and loyal aide, was given the task of delivering the news. He sat with the leader on the campaign bus and laid the scenario out.

Harris shook his head in disagreement. The polls were wrong, he said. They could not measure the popularity of individual members in their ridings. Bill Murdoch was running a strong campaign in Grey. Norm Sterling would hang on in Carleton. Chris Stockwell's popularity as alderman would serve him well in Etobicoke West. "I'll bet we can take twenty seats," he predicted.[1] Lindsay silently disagreed. The next night, in the face of the remarkable NDP upset of Peterson's government, the Tories secured their twenty seats—and a chance to fight again.

Harris may have had little polish, and he could never hope to sway the pundits and prognosticators who dominated the campuses and media outlets of southern Ontario, but he knew his constituency. The solid, rural Tory vote remained, its nineteenth-century Reform roots intact, even if its members now voted for a party with the name of its former opponents. But Harris knew something else. The true political base of power in Ontario had shifted from the cities, which had increasingly dominated the landscape for a century, to the suburban developments that ringed those cities—the 905, as they were called, after the telephone area code surrounding Toronto. For forty years their numbers had grown, though their voting patterns had mirrored those of the city centres, since the interests of city and suburb were seen as one. Now those interests were diverging. City dwellers called for increased state support for transit, public housing, and welfare, while suburbanites drove cars, owned their own homes, and paid the taxes that sustained those on the dole. They were ready, Harris and his advisers expected, to vote for low-tax, non-interventionist governments. If support from the 905 could be married to the rural core vote, a new suburban and rural conservative coalition would underpin a revived Progressive Conservative government.

Harris linked his own ambitions to those of a cadre of young, intellectual neo-conservative idealists led by corporate head-hunter Tom Long and political operative Leslie Noble. These advisers were in many ways the opposite of Harris: university educated, urban, and intensely ideological. Harris's conservatism was more intuitive, populist, and grass roots. But both wanted to lower taxes and deregulate the state, and they had stuck with the party when most others had abandoned it. The youthful ideologues also knew that Harris was more likely to appeal to voters than any one of them would. Harris and the Right Young Things forged their own coalition. Lindsay, Long, and Noble, together with insurance executive Alister Campbell, economist Mark Mullins, and several others, crafted the Common Sense Revolution, a twenty-three-page manifesto promising major cuts to income taxes, a balanced budget, a reining-in of welfare-state entitlements, tough education standards, and a slimmed-down bureaucracy. The document was dismissed by the media as too crude and too extremist for the cosmopolitan Ontario electorate. But critics in the newspapers and the universities had been largely insulated from the corporate downsizings, the loss in property values, the interest-rate hikes, and the general insecurity of the 1990s recession. In a community whose culture is its economy, the province's decline amounted to a spiritual crisis, with Bob Rae's NDP government offering convincing evidence that the ruling priesthood was in league with the devil.

On June 8, 1995, the ex-urban middle classes of Pickering and Nepean, Stoney Creek and Cambridge joined with their bedrock Reform counterparts in Orillia, Parry Sound, Peterborough, and Brockville to elect Mike Harris on faith, awarding the Progressive Conservatives 82 of 130 seats, with 45 per cent of the popular vote. Their faith was rewarded. Once in power, Harris displayed a relentless commitment to fulfilling the core principles of the Common Sense Revolution. Union leaders shut down cities in protest, public servants went on strike, teachers followed, tens of thousands of demonstrators filled the lawns of Queen's Park, enraged students smashed through the barricaded doors of the legislative building, and the opposition repeatedly paralysed the legislature. But Harris never wavered. His ministers ordered dozens of hospitals closed to save money, stripped school boards of their power and forced them to implement a tough new curriculum, slashed welfare benefits, and amalgamated municipal governments—most notoriously, those of Metropolitan Toronto. And Finance Minister Ernie Eves not only cut taxes but reformed the entire municipal property tax and assessment system.

The Conservatives considered their agenda a revolution—and most Ontarians emphatically agreed—simply because it shoehorned more than a generation's worth of reforms and restructuring into two and a half years of unremitting action. Harris's advisers were convinced they had to enact their mandate within the first half of the regime. "We can't put things off," Tony Clement, a future cabinet minister, confided early in the mandate, "because we'll get too close to an election and we'll lose our nerve."[2] Yet once in place, most of the Conservatives' reforms seemed to pay off. The turmoil and social costs notwithstanding, the election four years later—which all sides agreed would serve as a referendum on the results of the Common Sense Revolution—was actually a placid affair, with Harris slightly increasing his popular vote from the first majority government. Ontario had shaken off a generation of deficits and decline, fuelled by a renascent American economy and the latent benefits of free trade, which opened up the American market to Ontario entrepreneurs. Not only had the province modernized its crucial auto sector but it led the nation in the computer, communications, bio-technology, and other high-tech industries. After the speculative boom and disastrous collapse of property values in the 1980s, building and investment returned to the inner cities, even as the suburban edge cities continued to expand and proliferate. The deficit shrank along with the size of the state, disappearing altogether by the spring of 2000. The one promise that even the Tories' most ardent supporters expected not to be kept—the creation of 725,000 new jobs within five years—was met and exceeded. Ontario joined the economic motors of California, the Great Lakes, and the New South in leading North America through its longest and most stable period of expansion since the 1950s.

The social costs of this economic restructuring would be harder to measure and more contentious. Despite higher spending on health care, from $17 billion to $22 billion, emergency wards remained choked and cancer patients were increasingly being sent to the United States for treatment. Welfare rolls shrank by 40 per cent, but how many former recipients found jobs and how many ended up on the street remain matters of debate. Morale in the teaching profession became subterranean and, by the end of 2000, still showed no signs of improving. Overshadowing all else, Tory cuts to the Environment Ministry, and sloppy procedures while downloading responsibility for water treatment to municipalities, indirectly contributed to the death of seven people from contaminated water in the town of Walkerton in May 2000.

But whatever the long-term costs, social and political, of the Common Sense Revolution, no one would disagree that Harris's success in his first term left him politically stronger than any of his recent predecessors as premier. On the last day of the 1999 campaign, a handful of desultory protesters greeted him at a party rally in Orillia. Harris appeared to ignore the jeers of the demonstrators as he made his way to his campaign bus, but, as he stepped into the coach, he suddenly turned and waved. The protestors howled in impotent defiance. Harris waved back, his ear-to-ear grin an unmistakable declaration of victory—and derision. This was the real Mike Harris: confident, arrogant, determined to win at all costs, contemptuous of his enemies.

This was the Mike Harris who confronted Jean Chrétien.

The return of the Tories to power in Ontario should have been good news for the Liberals in Ottawa. The federation always worked best when opposite parties inhabited Queen's Park and Parliament Hill.

Frost and St. Laurent; Davis and Trudeau; even Peterson and Mulroney, at least on constitutional matters. Things always seemed to deteriorate, however, when identical parties were in both first ministers' offices. John Diefenbaker had a testy relationship with Leslie Frost; Bill Davis's relations with Brian Mulroney were far less cordial than with Pierre Trudeau. And there were the epic confrontations between Mitch Hepburn and Mackenzie King.

Harris, committed to spending cuts in his own manifesto, had cautiously supported Paul Martin's slashing of provincial transfers and was solidly behind the expansion of free trade. Ontario would finally be singing from the same fiscal song book as the federal government, a duet that would do inestimable good to the nation's overall economic agenda. No more would the Bank of Canada have to jack up interest rates to counteract the inflationary actions of the Ontario finance minister. No more would Ontario continue pushing Canada towards the debt wall with its multi-billion-dollar deficits, even as Ottawa and other provinces reduced theirs. Further, with Ontario supportive of overall federal economic policy, the prime minister would be free to tackle the separatist threat in Quebec. The night after the election, Chrétien telephoned Harris to congratulate him on his victory. The premier-designate replied that he hoped the two governments would work cooperatively to meet the nation's pressing economic challenges. Things seemed to be off to a good start.

But beneath the superficial optimism lay deeper fissures, ones that were bound to strain the relationship of leaders with even the best of intentions. In part, it was a question of ideology. Although sections of the economic underpinning of the Common Sense Revolution matched the federal Liberal agenda, the provincial program went considerably farther, promising tax cuts as well as spending and deficit cuts. The Liberals in Ottawa were determined to slay the deficit monster first, before tackling the taxation issue. Indeed, during the initial six years of the Liberal administration, taxes stealthily rose, thanks to the absence of indexation. By freezing the income level at which people moved into a higher tax, thousands of Canadians each year were pushed into the next bracket as their salaries rose through inflation. During the 1995 provincial election campaign, when Liberal leader Lyn McLeod appeared at first to enjoy a commanding lead in the polls—a provincial Liberal wag once joked: "Our party is always the most popular party, except for a couple of weeks every four years or so when, unfortunately, there's an election"—Paul Martin appeared at Queen's Park to endorse his provincial counterpart's economic platform and to trash the Tories'. "You can't have a massive tax cut across the board at the same time you're talking about deficit reduction unless what you're prepared to do is abandon your social responsibilities,"[3] he maintained. The problem, as several editorialists mentioned, was that McLeod's platform also contained promises of tax cuts. Martin was not, in truth, defending the provincial Liberals' policies so much as his own.

Then there was the question of federal transfers. Harris had been compelled to support the slashing of benefits to Ontario, since he was cutting spending himself. But the form that the federal cuts took soon rankled. By rolling all existing transfers into a single Canada Health and Social Transfer, Martin had incorporated the cap on CAP that discriminated against Ontario into the transfer, forcing the province to pay the lion's share of its welfare costs. It also didn't take the Tories long to mimic the NDP in protesting against the federal Employment Insurance policy, in which provincial contributions grossly exceeded benefits to unemployed Ontario workers.

Moreover, all provincial governments were becoming increasingly restive over Ottawa's determination to impose standards in the delivery of social policy, even as it cut its own financial contribution. In Alberta, Premier Ralph Klein threatened to go without federal money, after Ottawa warned it would cut transfers to the province unless it abandoned its policy of permitting private clinics for some medical services. In British Columbia, NDP premier Mike Harcourt offered the same warning after the federal government insisted he could not impose residency requirements on citizens receiving welfare benefits. Both governments ultimately retreated, but the controversies forewarned of crises to come as the federal spending power declined while its determination to maintain national standards continued. And when those crises arrived, Ontario would be making the same claims, only with a bigger economy to back up its demands.

Ultimately, the Chrétien and Harris governments were bound to clash—they were competing for the souls of Ontario voters. The federal Liberals held 97 of the 99 Ontario seats in the House of Commons. Ontario was the Liberal Party's great bastion, the source of its majority. But the same voters who supported the Liberals in Ottawa on September 8, 1993, also supported the Conservatives in Toronto on June 8, 1995. Voters were attracted to and supported two political parties that, while sharing a commitment to economic restraint, disagreed fundamentally over tax cuts and social policy. If the voters ever came to accept the provincial Conservative philosophy over the federal Liberal one, the future of the Chrétien government would be in grave jeopardy.

From the very beginning, then, Mike Harris was, potentially, Jean Chrétien's most dangerous foe.

Still, the Conservatives tried, at least at first, to stay out of federal-provincial intrigues. Harris wanted to keep a polite but friendly distance from the nation's squabbles while he focused on this revolutionary domestic agenda. Arriving mere weeks after his election at the annual premiers' conference in St. John's, the rookie Ontario premier adopted a low profile as the other first ministers tried to entice Jacques Parizeau, the separatist premier of Quebec, into joining them in their campaign to win more funds and powers from Ottawa.

Yet, although he kept his head down, Harris made two points to the premiers that would serve as the pillars of his administration's intra-Canadian policy. First, Ontario was in solidarity with the other provinces in demanding greater freedoms to manage social programs. Second, Ontario would oppose any federal policy that gave one province new powers or freedoms not enjoyed by other provinces. At the conference, the nine English-speaking premiers—Parizeau walked out after the other premiers warned him that a separate Quebec could not assume it would enjoy free trade with the rest of Canada—pledged to negotiate among themselves a common set of standards in health care, education, and welfare that could serve as provincially generated national standards. The resolution served as a dangerous warning to Ottawa that the provinces were ready to forge their own agreement on social policy, with or without federal participation.

But Ottawa's attentions were focused elsewhere, on the perennial problem of Quebec. Parizeau was determined to hold a second referendum on independence. He set a date of October 30, with a clumsily worded resolution that would give the Quebec government authority to negotiate with Canada for Quebec's sovereignty and to proclaim it independently if negotiations failed. At first, the sovereigntists seemed doomed: Parizeau was an unpopular leader, a pretentious stuffed shirt with English mannerisms and a dangerously interventionist economic philosophy. But part way through the campaign he reluctantly handed leadership over to Lucien Bouchard, a former cabinet minister in the Mulroney government who had split from the Conservative Party after the Meech Lake fiasco and formed his own sovereigntist Bloc Québécois at the federal level. Bouchard's political daring, coupled with his brooding charisma, captivated voters, and support for the sovereigntist side surged. The paucity of ideas and leadership in the federalist campaign was suddenly exposed. Chrétien could not compete with Bouchard in emotional appeal in Quebec, as Trudeau had competed with Lévesque. The federal cuts to transfers had weakened the argument that Quebec would suffer without federal support. In the end, the No side could offer only an emotional appeal: "We love you. Don't leave." It proved just barely enough.

Harris himself, along with his son Mike Jr., attended the rally in Montreal on the eve of the referendum in which tens of thousands of Canadians, many from outside the province, urged Quebecers not to forsake the federation. The last-minute emotional surge pushed back the sovereigntist tide, earning the No forces the narrowest of victories over the Yes, 49.7 per cent to 48.5 per cent, with 1.8 per cent of the ballots spoiled. It was a close call and it appalled Jean Chrétien, who came within a hair of being the prime minister who lost Quebec. In the dying days of the campaign he promised a new relationship between Quebec and the rest of Canada. The vote was barely in when he set about trying to make the promise come true.

Two mornings after the referendum, the prime minister and the Ontario premier met in secret in a Toronto hotel room, so Harris could hear Chrétien's plans for appeasing Quebec. Harris didn't want the meeting. To begin with, he had the flu and was feeling miserable. More important, the Ontario premier remained determined not to see his economic and social agenda derailed over constitutional finagling. Besides, Harris flatly opposed Chrétien's plans.

The Liberal prime minister was convinced that Quebec needed and deserved two guarantees under the constitution to protect its unique position within Confederation: recognition that the francophone province was a distinct society, although that distinction did not override the Charter of Rights and Freedoms; and a veto against any future constitutional change that Quebec decided offended its interests. To entrench these two guarantees in the constitution, Chrétien needed the consent of seven provinces representing 50 per cent of the population. Newfoundland, Alberta, and British Columbia were out of the question, Chrétien concluded; all three premiers and their constituencies were adamant that Quebec should not be offered any distinct privileges not shared by other provinces. But the three Maritime provinces could be brought onside, Chrétien reasoned, along with Saskatchewan and Manitoba. That left Ontario. If Harris would agree to support the constitutional amendment, Chrétien would have six provinces. The prime minister could then present Bouchard—now certain to be premier after Parizeau's decision to resign in the wake of the referendum result and his unfortunate remarks about "money and the ethnic vote" sabotaging the result—with an uncomfortable choice: sign on to the proposed new constitutional deal or reject the essence of everything Quebec had been demanding throughout the Meech and Charlottetown rounds. Chrétien had reason to hope the rookie Ontario premier could be counted on. The Ontario legislature, after all, had unanimously affirmed a motion during the referendum crisis recognizing Quebec's "distinct character within our country."

But Chrétien hoped in vain. Harris shook his head as the prime minister made his impassioned plea for Ontario's aid in constitutional reform. "Jean, I tell you as a friend, it's a mistake,"[4] he replied. The premier was convinced the federal response was demonstrably panicky and would upset the rest of the country without placating Quebec. He was already on record as promising no constitutional change without a referendum in Ontario. And Ontario's premier would never sanction a constitutional veto for Quebec without a similar weapon for Ontario. He had signalled his conviction at St. John's that no province, including Quebec, should be entitled to any benefit or power within Confederation not also given to the other provinces. If Quebec had a veto, then Ontario should have one too, along with the western provinces and Atlantic Canada. He knew his suburban and rural constituency had no stomach for constitutional wrangling, and certainly no interest in seeing Quebec receive preferential treatment over Ontario. He had no interest himself.

"Can I count on your support?" Chrétien pressed.

"No," Harris replied, flatly.

The fallout from that morning spread like a stain on the waters of the federation, fouling the relations between the Ontario and the federal governments, with consequences that would ultimately reshape federal-provincial powers to Ottawa's detriment. A personal breach also formed between Chrétien and Harris, with neither man, nor his advisers, ever fully trusting the other again.

Without Harris's support, Chrétien had no choice but to proceed unilaterally. Several weeks later the prime minister proposed federal legislation that would affirm Quebec's status as a distinct society, while providing Quebec, Ontario, the Atlantic provinces collectively, and the West collectively with a veto over constitutional changes. As well, the federal government would transfer responsibility for labour training programs to the provinces, a long-standing Quebec demand. The hasty and ill-considered proposal raised a firestorm of protest in British Columbia, a Pacific province that had virtually nothing in common with the three Prairie provinces to which it would be yoked in a single veto. After a week of relentless pressure, Chrétien surrendered and promised British Columbia a veto too. The Parti Québécois responded that if everyone had a veto, then it was worthless and Quebec had gained nothing. The prime minister's determination to proceed alone seemed only to have made the constitutional mess worse.

In fact, Ottawa was gravely weakened, as almost everyone in the federal cabinet recognized. The Liberals had only barely held back a vote for Quebec secession and were now less popular in Quebec than their sovereigntist opponents. The cuts to federal spending, and the deficit crisis that had spawned those cuts, had not only undermined Ottawa's ability to influence social policy but compromised its ability to act in areas of its own jurisdiction. To cut costs, Chrétien's government had already moved to hand over ownership of the nation's major airports to private companies, and to offload responsibility for ports to local agencies. It had sliced a billion dollars from the budget of the Canadian Broadcasting Corporation and cut the budget for VIA Rail to the bone. It had continued the decades-long downsizing of the Canadian military, slashing the Defence budget by 23 per cent, reducing the already emaciated regular troop strength from 75,000 to 59,000, and cancelling plans to replace the 1960s-vintage Sea King helicopters. Ottawa, in other words, was having increasing difficulty in exercising authority within its own areas of jurisdiction, much less projecting power into the jurisdictions of the provinces. And, as the tumult of the Quebec referendum receded and the ordinary business of the Confederation resumed, Ottawa found itself ever more preoccupied with a new and dangerous challenge: an aggressive and independent-minded Ontario.

The Harris government's belligerent posture towards Ottawa had no philosophical root. If Mike Harris has ever devoted significant time to thinking carefully through his own views on the role of Ontario as a dominant region within a federal state, he has yet to reveal the results. In placing Dianne Cunningham—a former leadership rival conspicuously outside his trusted inner ring of advisers and ministers—in the role of intergovernmental affairs minister, a portfolio that both Rae and Peterson had kept for themselves, he was consciously distancing himself from the whole affair.

Ernie Eves, Harris's powerful finance minister and close personal friend, likewise brought no sophisticated new thinking to Ontario's role in the nation's fiscal or monetary matrix. David Lindsay, Guy Giorno, and Deb Hutton, the most influential advisers within the premier's office, at first thought little and cared less about federal or interprovincial affairs. To the extent that Harris personally, or his administration collectively, contemplated its role in the federation, its position was simple: Ontario would willingly do its duty to Confederation by supporting less fortunate regions through equalization payments, a time-honoured act of Christian charity that the government was happy to maintain. Further, the Harris government not only accepted the principle of free trade but embraced it. The province would encourage and endorse any moves to lower non-tariff barriers within the economic union, just as it encouraged the lowering of those barriers between Canada and the rest of the world. Finally, Harris held to a pragmatic belief that the level of government that provided a service should also be the level of government that funded it and administered it. (This philosophy would be invoked to justify the massive Who Does What restructuring of provincial and municipal responsibilities in 1997.) Otherwise, Ontario was happy to be left alone to pursue its destiny, wishing the other parts of Canada well as they pursued theirs.

Except, as the Ontario Tories increasingly discovered, this seemingly innocuous live-and-let-live policy actively threatened the federal government's very reason for being. One of Ottawa's fundamental roles—indeed, its most fundamental role, as its relevance shrinks in its other areas of jurisdiction—is redistributing the wealth of the nation. Through the income tax and social programs, the government redistributes wealth from high-income earners to low. Through its transfer programs, it redistributes wealth from the affluent regions of the country—principally Ontario, but also Alberta and British Columbia—to the less developed. The conditions and incentives attached to that redistribution help the federal government to influence economic and social development throughout the country. Equalization payments, the only area of transfer that Ontario accepts as legitimate, are but one, and by no means the most important, of its tools.

One of the purposes of Employment Insurance (the Liberals' think-positive new name for Unemployment Insurance) was to siphon money from regions of low unemployment—principally Ontario—and direct the funds to benefits and training programs in regions of high unemployment, especially Atlantic Canada. The purpose of the cap on CAP, incorporated into the Canada Health and Social Transfer, was to lower the per capita federal payment for welfare to the wealthier provinces—Ontario, again—while sustaining them in the poorer provinces. Virtually everything the federal government does is done in the interests of redistribution, of tapping the wealth of the functional parts of the federation to create "national standards," in the form of subsidies to the dysfunctional parts. Harris and his advisers had not originally grasped this *raison d'être* of the federal government. When its truth quickly became clear, they reacted with indignation and an increasing determination to resist. In this, Harris was simply retracing the voyage of self-discovery that his predecessor, Bob Rae, had already undertaken. But while Rae had railed futilely from a weak political and economic base, Harris confronted Chrétien from a position of political strength in a province whose economy was literally being transformed. Even in the darkest days of the provincewide teachers' strike of autumn 1997, the premier's popularity never slipped below the mid-thirties mark.

Ontarians, more than any other Canadians, expect their province to be prosperous. The primacy of progress is nowhere more fundamentally embraced than in the Laurentian lowlands; the enervation and decline that threatened the province's economy in the 1970s and devastated it in the early 1990s made people wonder what had gone wrong, what they had done to lose their way. But the restructuring forced on the province by free trade and the recession was starting, by 1994, to produce results. Growth in that year reached a healthy 5.5 per cent. It shuddered again in early 1995, dropping down to 2.5 per cent, as the continuing drag of deficits, taxes, and high interest rates continued to act as a chronic brake. But the stern cuts to spending that the Tories launched in July 1995 and the tax cuts that began in 1996, aiding and abetting the blissful fallout of the American boom, set the economy back on the rails. Ontario surged ahead in 1997 with a growth rate of 4.8 per cent and, by 1999, had confounded all forecasts with a growth rate of 5.9 per cent. Unemployment declined steadily from 9.6 per cent in 1994 to well under 6 per cent in 1999. In some sectors, especially construction and high technology, labour shortages emerged as a growing problem. Spurred on by reduced benefits and more jobs, the welfare caseload plummeted by more than one-third, from 669,000 in 1994 to 430,000 in 1999.

The revived Ontario economy was not only bigger but different. Without tariff barriers, the compass of the manufacturing and service sectors swung emphatically to north-south from east-west. In 1989, the first full year after the Free Trade Agreement went into effect, foreign exports (90 per cent of them to the United States) made up only 30 per cent of Ontario's gross domestic product. By 1999 the figure had reached 54 per cent. The people in Oakville and Oshawa, Alliston and Cambridge knew why. Our lower dollar encouraged the reviving American automotive industry to upgrade and invest in its Canadian operations. The province's auto assembly capacity increased by 26 per cent between 1996 and 1999, causing experts to predict that Ontario would soon surpass Michigan as North America's leading auto-manufacturing centre. But it wasn't all, or even mostly, about cars. Ontario-based Nortel helped push the Ontario economy and the Toronto Stock Exchange to record heights, as the telecommunications industry led the provincial economy in growth. While low–technology-based industries such as automobiles grew at an average rate of 4 per cent between 1997 and 2000, the high-technology sector posted annual growth rates as high as 15 per cent. Even rust-belt industries such as steel rebounded. Manufacturers great and small exploited the opportunity afforded by the newly accessible American market.

Once again, a province built on wheat, and transformed into a modern industrial state by automobiles, refashioned itself in preparation for the next millennium. In Ottawa the quiet west-end suburb of Kanata became the centre of Canada's burgeoning high-technology sector: local developers frantically converted shopping malls to office space to accommodate dot.coms starved for room to expand. Vacancy rates became a fiction, growing even tighter than

Toronto's. There, the return of good times dissipated the hole-in-the-doughnut fears for the downtown. Although the Tories' tough welfare laws, abolition of new subsidized housing, and underfunding of psychiatric services probably contributed to the blight of homeless beggars on the city's streets and the squeegee kids who harassed its motorists (at least until the Tories made involuntary windshield-washing illegal), other signs pointed to a Toronto reborn: the trendy new restaurants of College West, the proliferation of rundown warehouses converted to upscale condominiums, the crowds that clogged Bloor Street on a Saturday afternoon. Almost everywhere across the province the tale was the same: the tattered main street of Chatham showed new signs of life, refurbished resorts thrived once again in Muskoka, the boom-and-bust cycle of Sudbury settled into a steadier prosperity. Demand for housing was so high that the biggest problem was finding workers and materials to meet demand. The crowds of protesters who fought against the Tory tide during the first term evaporated, replaced on the lawns of Queen's Park by Asian tourists videotaping the voracious squirrels. The teachers, sullen, accepted their swollen workloads but refused to lead after-school activities such as soccer and band practice. The laidoff public servants had surprisingly little difficulty finding new jobs. Only the very unskilled could find no work in a province that, by 2001, was showing pronounced signs of a labour shortage. Ontario was back.

Its return had profound implications for Ontario's relations with Ottawa and the rest of Canada. As falling commodity prices and the exhausted fisheries threatened the economies of the West and Atlantic Canada, and chronic uncertainty about its future hampered Quebec's growth, Ottawa became ever more dependent on revenues from Ontario's private and corporate taxpayers. But since its fundamental role was to act as an agency of redistribution, and the need was so great elsewhere, Ottawa was neither inclined nor able to reward the economic heartland for its munificence. On the contrary, transfers out of Ontario to the rest of the country increased. And the traditional argument that the dollars returned to Ontario as they stimulated purchases of Ontario-made goods by consumers elsewhere no longer washed, even if it had been true in the first place. The Ontario economy was now oriented firmly north-south. The province did more than $50 billion in trade with Michigan alone. The spending power of American consumers meant far more to Ontario's assembly lines than the inclinations of Winnipeggers to buy a watch containing Sudbury nickel. If transfers really did stimulate other markets to purchase Ontario goods, the province's interests would have been better served by sending the money to Tennessee.

The economic bonds between Ontario and the rest of the country had weakened dramatically. The Ontario Conservative government was well to the right of the federal Liberal government. Mike Harris believed in special treatment for no province and the disentangling of federal and provincial responsibilities. His government opposed any transfers from the Ontario taxpayer to other regions outside the framework of equalization grants. The disastrous meeting in November 1995 diminished his opinion of Chrétien's political acumen.

The federal government, nevertheless, was determined to use all the tools at its disposal to redistribute wealth from Ontario to the rest of the country. The Liberals were not prepared to cede their influence in the area of spending power on social programs, especially in health care. Chrétien resented the tax-cutting policies of the Ontario government as irresponsible and as a challenge to his own government's determination to emphasize deficit reduction. He felt Harris had let him down after the referendum by not agreeing to cooperate in constitutional reform.

Things were bound to get ugly.

It started, predictably enough, with taxes. Since the First World War, provincial governments have fought with Ottawa over what they saw as its theft of the power to tax income. But Ottawa's control of the income-tax system was aggravating for other reasons as well, as Finance Minister Ernie Eves quickly discovered. When provincial governments finally began to tax income, they simply calculated their taxes as a percentage of the federal tax, leaving Ottawa to define taxable income and the various tax tiers. Revenue Canada also collected all the income taxes and then remitted the provincial portion back to the provinces. (Quebec, always the exception, directly set and collected its own tax.) Eves, however, wanted to create a special surtax on incomes over $50,000—the Fair Share Health Care Levy—which would be based directly on income. Revenue Canada quickly scotched the idea: provinces had to base their taxes on federal taxes, if they wanted the federal government to collect them. Ontario reluctantly converted its proposed levy into a regular surtax.

The Goods and Services Tax also emerged as an irritant. Chrétien had made a rash promise during the 1993 election campaign to scrap the hated GST. Now, two years into the mandate, the impossibility of that pledge was obvious to everyone, not least the prime minister and the minister of finance. But the GST could *appear* to be scrapped if it were harmonized with the existing provincial sales taxes into a single tax with a different name.

The federal and Quebec governments, in a rare moment of cooperation, had agreed in 1991 to blend their taxes, with Quebec responsible for collecting it. The Atlantic provinces, with the exception of Prince Edward Island, were also willing to harmonize their provincial sales taxes with the GST. And Ernie Eves, soon after being sworn in as finance minister, announced that Ontario would harmonize the PST and the GST as well. Harmonization was in accord with the Tory government's policy of cutting down on paperwork.

But when Ottawa negotiated the Harmonized Sales Tax in 1996 with the Atlantic provinces, it agreed as well to a $1 billion subsidy, allegedly to compensate for new goods that would be taxed, and to offset the costs of harmonization. Really, it was just another transfer. This deal enraged Quebec, which had signed on without compensation, and Alberta, which has no provincial sales tax and would therefore never be eligible for a subsidy.

The Atlantic HST did not go down well with Ontario either. Ottawa was offering the province none of the harmonization subsidies it was offering Atlantic Canada. What's more, the GST applied to services as well as goods, and harmonizing the tax would actually increase the burden on taxpayers by about $3 billion. "Hell would freeze over" before Ontario would sign such an accord, Harris declared, pulling the plug on negotiations.[5]

But it was the federal revenue grab of Ontario taxes that most annoyed Queen's Park. As the Conservatives attempted to reconcile their determination to cut taxes with their equal determination to restructure the health care, education, and municipal sectors, they became increasingly chagrined by the money that was flowing out of the province into the pockets of others, in particular through Employment Insurance. It was galling that, by 1997, the EI reserve had reached a more-than-comfortable $12 billion. To make matters worse, Finance Minister Paul Martin was proposing a steep new tax, in the form of increased Canada Pension Plan contributions, to top up the underfunded pension scheme. Harris strongly opposed increased CPP contributions, especially when the Employment Insurance fund enjoyed such a huge surplus. Martin, however, was loath to cut EI premiums, which he counted on to help reduce the federal deficit. Under the original CPP agreement, the provincial governments had to consent before the federal government could raise premiums. Harris publicly announced that Ontario would withhold consent to any increase in CPP contributions without an equivalent cut to EI premiums. After months of protracted negotiations, Martin agreed to slightly lower EI premiums in exchange for the CPP premium increase. In the short term, the cut and the increase would cancel each other out. But cutting premiums failed to address the larger issue of Employment Insurance imbalance.

The shocks over federal tax policy were part of a painful awakening by the Harris administration throughout 1996 and 1997 to the uniquely disadvantaged place of Ontario within Confederation. The Tories had attributed Bob Rae's demands for "Fair Share Federalism" to the whines of a desperate premier looking for someone to blame for the province's woes. But as the Tories' attempts to close hospitals, find doctors for underserviced areas, expand long-term and community care, and save money ran into the bottlenecks of emergency-room line-ups, neo-natal bed shortages, and militant doctors, the implications of federal funding, or lack of it, coupled with federal regulations, began to chafe. Ottawa had once funded half of the health care costs of the province. By 1998 it was down to 11 per cent. In 1985 federal payments accounted for 17 per cent of provincial revenues. By 1998 the figure was down to 8 per cent. Yet Ottawa continued to tie its funding to strict conditions, such as the ban on extra billing by doctors or on residency by welfare recipients.

Shared-cost programs had turned out to be a mistake for Confederation. They hampered the provincial governments' ability to tailor their social programs to each province's individual needs, while imposing on provincial governments federal restrictions that weren't justified by federal involvement. In Harris's mind, as the drawbacks of the status quo became increasingly glaring, two conclusions emerged: the federal and provincial governments needed to clarify Who Does What in each area of jurisdiction; and the provinces, which are fundamentally responsible for health, education, and welfare, could probably do a better job than the federal government in setting national standards in these areas.

At first, Chrétien seemed to agree. Weakened by its cuts to programs, shaken by the near loss of Quebec in the 1995 referendum, and unwilling to face an increasingly united front of hostile provinces, the Liberals in the 1996 Speech from the Throne promised major concessions to the provinces. The federal government, Governor General Romeo LeBlanc revealed, was willing to retreat from a broad range of jurisdictions, including forestry, the environment, tourism, and, most important, labour training, handing responsibility over to the provinces. The federal government was also prepared to agree not to introduce any future spending programs in areas of provincial jurisdiction without the consent of the provincial governments. And Chrétien was as good as his word. At a first ministers' conference in Ottawa in June 1996 the prime minister signed an agreement handing over the jurisdictions named in the Throne Speech to the provinces, subject to negotiated agreements with each province in the area of labour training. But, as it turned out, the provincial governments already had a much bigger power grab in mind. Two months after the Ottawa summit, the premiers met in Jasper, Alberta, for what would turn out to be perhaps the most important premiers' conference in the country's history.

Harris arrived at the meeting with a paper that the Ontario government had commissioned from Thomas Courchene. Ever since the failure of Meech, the Queen's University political economist had been arguing that greater autonomy for the provinces was inevitable, in light of the alienation of the West and the failure of conventional federalism to accommodate the aspirations of Quebec. Courchene, however, was convinced that Quebec and the West were not the only regions failing to benefit from the existing federation. Ontario, he believed, needed to reconsider its role, given the economic restructuring brought on by free trade and the punitive transfers being imposed on Ontario by the federal government. Now the academic's abstract theories were becoming concrete policy. Harris, at war with Ottawa over taxation, the pension plan, unemployment insurance, and federal cuts to transfers, agreed that Ontario, and all the provinces, needed a new deal within Confederation. That deal Courchene outlined in a paper co-sponsored by Ontario and Alberta "for discussion" by the premiers, a paper acronymically entitled *ACCESS: A Convention on the Canadian Economic and Social Systems*. Courchene urged the premiers to consider either a partial or a full reconstruction of the federation. Under a partial restructuring, Ottawa would surrender its authority to set national standards in social policy, with a joint federal-provincial council taking its place. In a full restructuring, the federal government would abandon any responsibility for social policy at all, with the provinces setting and maintaining standards through mutual consent.

ACCESS alarmed most of the premiers. As well as getting out of the social policy field, the paper proposed that the federal government be prohibited from any kind of transfers from have to have-not provinces, except for equalization payments. The Atlantic provinces, Saskatchewan, and Manitoba saw their federal supports disappearing, with powerful Ontario and Alberta dominating—and even bullying—the poorer provinces in the provincial council. They flatly rejected the proposal during a preliminary discussion on a train ride from Edmonton to Jasper, the conference site. "We threw Courchene off the train," Newfoundland premier Brian Tobin quipped to reporters. But Courchene was not so easily dispatched. Within a matter of months, at a supplementary meeting in Calgary, the nine English-speaking premiers had agreed to much of what he proposed.

The logic was simply too compelling. Even the poorest of provinces chafed at the injustice of a federal government that no longer paid for social programs, but dictated their principles. There is an inevitable correlation between money and power in politics; over time, the two must coalesce. Ottawa had been retreating on its funding of social programs for more than a decade; the loss of its authority to dictate those programs' principles could be delayed, but not prevented. Further, the English Canadian premiers all agreed that the provinces needed to offer their own response to the near calamity of the Quebec referendum. Federal leadership of the issue, after all, had nearly proved ruinous. This was an astonishing assertion of authority: the English provinces saw themselves as equally legitimate with the federal government in meeting the challenge of French separatism.

And so the Calgary Declaration, released by a united front of English Canadian premiers in Calgary in September 1997, represented a double-edged assertion of the determination of the provincial premiers to rebalance the federation, both by transferring new powers to the provincial governments (in fact, restoring powers that had been slowly ebbing since the Second World War) and by asserting the right of the provincial governments to determine the standards in social policy they were responsible for implementing. The declaration's seven principles affirmed, once again, the special right of the Quebec government to protect the French language and culture within Confederation, but insisted that any power granted to one province must be granted to all alike, and that the federal government must act only in cooperation with the provincial governments when attempting to establish programs in the field of provincial responsibility.

The remarkable unanimity among the English-speaking premiers resulted not simply from the obvious mutuality of interest in winning these new powers, but in the 180-degree reversal by the Ontario government. Under Davis, even under Peterson, Ontario would never have joined the other provinces to present a united front against Ottawa. Now, under Harris, Ontario was not only onside but actually leading the charge, working with Klein's Alberta to convince the other provinces to fight for their greater autonomy. For the smaller provinces, the risks of losing Ontario-paid transfers under a rebalanced federation was less than the risk of estranging Ontario. For as history had proved, if Ontario and Quebec together decided to oppose the federal power, the federal power usually had to give. Ontario and Quebec, united, had wrested powers from the central government after Confederation. They had asserted the right of the provinces to develop their own hydroelectric power. They had stymied federal attempts at constitutional reform in the days of Duplessis and Hepburn. They had checked the acquisitiveness of Ottawa in taxation at the 1947 first ministers' conference.

Now Harris was speaking a language dangerously similar in substance, if not in tone, to the sovereigntist rhetoric of Lucien Bouchard. Harris and Bouchard, who became well acquainted during the 1996 Team Canada trade mission of first ministers, were known to like each other personally, as did their wives—a marked contrast to the frigid relationship between the prime minister and the two premiers. And there was much in the Calgary Declaration that a sovereigntist in Quebec could support, in both the downloading of responsibilities and the limitation of the federal power. If the smaller provinces had ignored Ontario's assertive new stance, Bouchard and Harris might well have responded by uniting with Alberta and British Columbia to demand their own new deal. The four largest provinces of Confederation would then be arrayed against Ottawa and the smaller provinces. The other provincial premiers, calculating the balance of forces, opted to side with the Big Three provinces, a telling indication of where they felt power lay.

The Calgary Declaration posed an exquisite dilemma for Prime Minister Chrétien. He had already acceded to the idea of handing over a broad range of powers to the provincial governments, in tacit admission of his own government's diminished role. Now the provinces were demanding increased powers in the crucial field of social policy. If the federal government could not portray itself as the national guardian of the welfare state, protecting its citizens from coast to coast from the avarice of petty provincial politicians, what role would be left for it in the lives of its citizens? And, indeed, Chrétien brusquely rejected any suggested compromise, especially in the area of health care. "If we abandon enforcement, you abandon Medicare," Chrétien told reporters shortly after the premiers' declaration. "That's why we have a national government that makes sure that services are to a certain level across the land."[6]

The Calgary Declaration required an answer, and it could not simply be a flat no. To reject the united resolution of the English Canadian provinces, even as Ottawa attempted to contain Quebec, would leave the federal government utterly isolated, without an ally in Confederation. Chrétien clearly had no reason to believe that Canadians would rally to Ottawa's side. In the West and in Quebec, those leaders were reacting to the visceral resentment of the federal power expressed by their own citizens—and now the Ontario government was joining them. If the Liberal Party rejected the Calgary Declaration, in essence rejecting Harris's demands for greater autonomy and control for his province, Chrétien would be asking the very voters who sustained his government to choose between Queen's Park or Parliament Hill. Perhaps their first loyalty would still be to Ottawa: polls consistently showed that Ontarians identified themselves as Canadians more than citizens in other parts of the country. But it would be a dangerous gamble. How could the federal government or the Liberal Party hope to emerge strengthened from the contest?

Reluctantly, Chrétien decided he had to deal. After stalling for more than a year, while Ottawa and the provinces wrangled over the mechanics of downloading job training and a national child benefit, the prime minister agreed at a December 1997 first ministers' conference to begin negotiating a federal-provincial "social union." Just what this social union would represent, both sides disagreed on from the moment the process began. Provincial premiers, including Harris, envisioned, *à la* Calgary, joint federal-provincial control of existing social programs, including possible revisions to the Canada Health Act, coupled with strict prohibitions on the federal government creating any new programs without provincial consent. And that was what Chrétien agreed to put on the table for discussion during the day-long first ministers' meeting. But Health Minister

Allan Rock almost torpedoed the entire scheme when, during the afternoon session, he told waiting reporters that revisions to the Canada Health Act would not be negotiable. The premiers, Harris especially, were furious. Chrétien had explicitly agreed that health care was on the table. Now Rock was taking it off. On this note, negotiations among Dianne Marleau, the federal minister of intergovernmental affairs, and her provincial counterparts began.

But political dialogue rarely, if ever, occurs in a vacuum, and the atmosphere of the social union discussions quickly became contaminated by a new feud between Jean Chrétien and Mike Harris, one that eclipsed all others in bitterness. The issue was tainted blood, and it would produce a kind of internal cold war that left Ottawa-Ontario relations more dysfunctional than at any time since the wild and woolly days of Mitch Hepburn and Mackenzie King.

Between 1980 and 1990 the Canadian blood supply, like that of other countries, became infected with HIV, the lethal virus that causes AIDS, and the hepatitis C virus. Hep C, as it was called, is a debilitating, incurable disease that can cause chronic fatigue, a weakened immune system, liver damage, and cancer. It can ultimately be fatal. Tens of thousands of Canadians were unknowingly infected with these diseases. When a test that could detect HIV became available in 1985, the Red Cross began screening the supply, although not until eight months after the United States had its screens in place. Through a combination of mismanagement and misunderstanding, the Red Cross took no action to protect against the presence of hep C, even though partially reliable tests were available. (It had been testing for hepatitis B since the early 1970s.) Finally, in 1990, with the arrival of a much more reliable test, screening procedures were put in place and the supply was purified. The discovery that the Red Cross, a name synonymous with competence and compassion, had permitted 20,000 people or more to become infected with hepatitis C, when that tragedy could have been at least partly avoided, was a national disgrace. In November 1997 an inquiry conducted by Justice Horace Krever recommended compensation for everyone who had been infected through the blood supply. Tragically, many of those infected with HIV did not live to see the end of the four-year inquiry. But most of those infected with hepatitis C were still very much alive, which was why both the federal and the provincial governments baulked at the recommendation. Full compensation would cost the governments billions of dollars at a time when they were struggling to eliminate their chronic deficits. Health Minister Rock immediately began discussions with his provincial counterparts to see what, if any, joint solution they could come up with.

When the question of compensation first emerged, the Ontario government was the most niggardly player at the table. Jim Wilson, the provincial health minister, insisted that his government would already be paying millions of dollars in health costs to treat those infected, and further compensation would be too costly. But public sympathy for the victims was enormous. After three months of protracted bargaining, Rock and the ten ministers agreed in March 1998 to a joint offer: the federal and provincial governments would provide $1.1 billion in compensation to the roughly 6,600 victims of hepatitis C infected between 1986 and 1990, when the Americans were already testing their blood supply for hep C but the Red Cross neglected to do so. Ottawa would provide $800 million, the largest chunk of compensation, with the rest to be shared by the other provinces, on a weighted basis. Ontario's contribution would be $113 million. (The provinces got off relatively lightly, on the grounds that their health care systems would be shouldering most of the treatment costs.) There would be no compensation for those infected before 1986, when Canada was deemed to have been no more negligent than most other nations in monitoring its blood supply.

The half-measures agreed to by the health ministers were roundly condemned from the moment they were announced. Hep C sufferers infected before 1986 had just as many needs as those infected after that date, and were suffering just as greatly. To them, and to the population at large, the 1986 cutoff seemed arbitrary and cruel. But, for once, the provinces and Ottawa stuck together. This was the best deal the governments could afford, Rock maintained, under relentless attack in the House of Commons from opposition MPs. On April 6 the health ministers issued a communiqué reaffirming their commitment: the federal and provincial governments felt they could weather the political storm, as long as they remained united on their deal. And perhaps they might have. Then, in one of the more breathtaking moments of political hardball—not to say opportunism—on record, Harris broke ranks.

Harris and his advisers always insisted that he changed his mind "because it was the right thing to do." They also maintained that Ontario misunderstood the nature of the initial agreement. The Ontario government had assumed, sources claimed, that hemophiliacs who had refused to receive blood transfusions because of suspicions that the blood supply might be tainted would also be compensated—for suffering caused by *not* having access to blood. But the agreement gave no compensation to these victims.

This was not an aspect of the debate that Health Minister Elizabeth Witmer or Mike Harris emphasized during the furor that followed. What was clear, however, was that the Canadian public was appalled by the deal. One poll (albeit one commissioned by the Canadian Hemophilia Society) stated that 87 per cent of Canadians felt that the federal and provincial governments had an obligation to extend full compensation. All politicians, then, were tainted by the agreement, and all were suffering in popularity.

The public rejection of the hep C accord was particularly dangerous for Harris. The premier's difficulties with health care were steadily mounting. Although he had avoided a strike by the province's doctors (by removing certain caps on their fees and backtracking on promises to require newly licensed doctors to move into underserviced areas), the strains of hospital restructuring had caused widespread anxiety. Newspaper headlines told of dying patients left on beds in hospital hallways, people receiving improper treatment from overstressed emergency departments, pregnant women shipped by ambulance from Toronto to Kingston because of the shortage of neo-natal beds, and cancer patients forced to seek treatment in the United States. In vain, Harris and Witmer protested that the ills of the province's health system had accumulated over decades. The public knew only that the government was shutting down hospitals. Opposition politicians accused the Tories of cutting the health care budget (in fact, it steadily increased each year), and voters were convinced that the Harris government was mishandling the file.

Harris had also just received a political black eye from the Dionne sisters. The three survivors of the famed Dionne quintuplets, who had attracted three million people to the North Bay area to watch their fish-bowl existence in the 1930s, were now living in poverty in Montreal. A publicist who took on their case maintained that the Ontario government, which had taken the children away from their parents and made them wards of the state, might have mishandled or even stolen the money the quints had earned during their famous childhood. Their cause was joined by the high-profile lawyer Clayton Ruby, who pressed for additional compensation both in the media and with Attorney General Charles Harnick. At first the government insisted that the Dionnes were owed nothing. Harnick and Harris, while adopting sympathetic tones, assured voters that the government's lawyers had examined the issue and concluded that the Dionnes had been given every cent to which they were entitled. This was hardly the politically appropriate response for a government already portrayed as hard-hearted and even cruel.

While the Conservative caucus met in Collingwood to plot strategy for the year before the 1999 election, the Dionne sisters appeared at Queen's Park with signs, demanding "justice, not charity." Public sympathy for the Dionnes was overwhelming. Harris and Harnick looked like Scrooges, and their phone lines were deluged with calls from angry voters. It took Harris a week before he surrendered, flying personally to Montreal to visit the sisters with a cake baked by his wife, Janet, and an offer of $4 million compensation. He ordered an inquiry into whether the quints had been financially exploited by the government, and left it to the sisters to decide whether the results should be kept secret or made public. The reversal was humiliating but instructive. It taught Harris that voters cared more about the moral perception of right and wrong than about legal niceties. And, as the Dionne affair quickly receded from the headlines, it also taught Harris that money could make all sorts of unpleasantness go away. It did not take his advisers long to bring to the premier's attention the parallel between the plight of the Dionnes and the plight of the victims of hepatitis C.

Those parallels were obvious: two groups, the object of public sympathy and remorse, were being deprived of compensation because of legal arguments that didn't wash with anyone outside government circles. Members of the public felt about the hep C victims as they felt about the Dionnes, and they were similarly disgusted with the government for abandoning these people. It was clear that if Ontario broke ranks with the other governments and extended compensation to the pre-1986 victims, it could reverse the political damage it was suffering and turn Harris into something he had never been thought of before: a compassionate politician. And the price was manageable; it would cost Ontario only an extra $200 million to extend compensation, a fraction of the reserve fund that Ernie Eves kept aside for exactly these contingencies. Of course, under the negotiated formula, Ottawa would be on the hook for as much as another billion dollars if the package were extended—but that was not Ontario's problem.

This disregard for the political ramifications to the federal government was Machiavellian in its pragmatism, but Harris didn't feel he owed Chrétien anything. Quite the opposite: the Ontario and federal governments were at odds over taxes, social policy, and how best to handle Quebec. In the preceding two years Chrétien had done nothing to make the Ontario premier feel grateful, and much to antagonize him. Having agreed to the social union negotiations in December, federal officials had not even bothered to set up schedules for meetings or exchanges of papers. Chrétien had no pull with Harris, and the Ontario premier felt no need to suffer along with the federal Liberals as the public condemned them for their deal. In fact, the Tories took some pleasure in it.

The opening came on April 29, when the Quebec National Assembly voted unanimously that the federal government should extend full compensation to all victims of hepatitis C infected through the blood supply. The next day Witmer, on an open-line radio program, concurred with Quebec. Once again, Ottawa was confronted with the scenario it always feared: a united Ontario-Quebec front, in this case forcing it to spend money it did not believe it could afford to spend. It was the old entente back again, after lying dormant for generations. Mowat and Mercier, Whitney and Lafontaine, Hepburn and Duplessis, Harris and Bouchard.

Through May the political crisis that the Ontario Tories had deliberately provoked heightened. Harris and Witmer sent their federal counterparts regular open letters, demanding that the federal government reopen negotiations to expand coverage. Occasionally Chrétien or Rock replied, to say the deal had been agreed to by all parties and was not subject to revision, although—in a pointed rebuke from one government to another—much of the time Ottawa simply ignored Ontario's missives. At the worst of it, on May 1, Harris and Chrétien were to meet in Brampton to celebrate expanded production at the Chrysler plant. The two men sat expressionless on the stage, studiously ignoring each other's presence. But when reporters questioned them separately afterward, an irritated and annoyed Chrétien lashed out at his tormentors. "[The provinces] are the ones who ran away from the deal," he maintained. "Under pressure by the press, they ran for cover ... I'm telling them, 'Hey, wait a minute. Put your money where your mouth is.'"[7] When Harris learned of Chrétien's comments, he lost his temper. Within days the Ontario government announced it was prepared unilaterally to extend compensation to all hep C victims in Ontario infected through the blood supply, regardless of the year.

Ontario's decision left the federal government in a deeply embarrassing situation. Reopening the deal was impossible for several reasons. Ottawa would be seen as surrendering to a health policy demand from a province. Ottawa would be far more financially liable than any one province—and the bill for the Health Department could conceivably swell to $2 billion. The poorer provinces, which were less able than Ontario to afford the extra compensation, would no doubt demand yet another subsidy from Ottawa, which Ontario would resist, since it would be paying part of the cost of it. The federal government refused to budge, even as the controversy degenerated into public relations ecstasy for the Ontario Tories and catastrophe for the federal Liberals. Hep C victims castigated the callous federal government while showering praise on Harris. Fifteen-year-old Joey Hache, a hep C victim who had bicycled across Canada to increase public pressure on Ottawa to extend compensation, visited Queen's Park to thank the beaming premier for fighting on behalf of his cause.

In a sense, it mattered more to Ontario than Ottawa. The Liberals had already won re-election in 1997 with a reduced majority, while Harris was going to the polls within a year. (And, indeed, Master Hache dutifully popped up during the 1999 election campaign to thank Harris once again.) The Liberals could count on the hep C controversy fading away over time, certainly by the next election. But it galled them to be painted as villains in the drama, to be unwilling pawns in boosting the popularity of what was turning into the most troublesome government in the federation—Quebec notwithstanding. It left Allan Rock indiscreetly vowing at a Liberal fundraising dinner in October 1998 that he and his fellow Liberals would "help in every way we can"[8] to defeat the Harris government in the next election, a remarkably partisan threat for a federal cabinet minister to make against an elected government. In the end, fearing to antagonize electors who seemed happy to vote for federal Liberals and provincial Conservatives simultaneously, and certain the Tories were headed for victory anyway, most federal Liberals stayed in the background during the campaign.

Rock's intemperate remarks hit the newspapers even as the intergovernmental affairs ministers were meeting in Edmonton in their latest attempt to hammer out a deal on the social union. The obstacle to the deal was apparent: the provincial governments were prepared to settle for nothing less than neutering the federal government in the social policy field. They wanted to impose joint federal-provincial control over the Canada Health Act and other social-policy legislation, and to prohibit the federal government from embarking on new programs in health, education, welfare, child care, or any other social field without provincial consent. The federal government was prepared to offer the provinces a consultative role in both regards, but not to retreat from the field entirely. And, to avoid being forced into a compromise, federal officials were doing everything possible to slow down the pace of negotiations by cancelling meetings and delaying reports.

The federal deficit was finally about to disappear, and the billions spent on eliminating it would be magically transformed into billions of dollars of surplus. The left wing of the Liberal caucus was determined to use the surplus to reinvigorate social policy, perhaps with a new national daycare program. Now was not the time to sign away the rights to launch those programs, whether the provinces wanted them or not. Paul Martin provocatively signalled exactly that intent in his 1998 budget when he announced the Millennium Scholarships, to be awarded to postsecondary students in financial need. Quebec, in particular, immediately denounced the scholarships as yet another illegitimate intrusion into its jurisdiction. The prospect that social union might forever put an end to such intrusions actually convinced Bouchard at the August 1998 premiers' conference in Saskatoon to join the final leg of negotiations aimed at reaching a deal.

Ultimately, the social union talks proved both a threat to and an opportunity for the federal government. Chrétien had to avoid surrendering so much power that the federal government would become unable to influence national policy. That meant he had to negotiate a compromise with the provinces on the social union that left Ottawa with something to do. To do that, he had to offer the Ontario and Alberta governments, both of which were essentially hostile to his administration, something in exchange. The political travails of BC Premier Glen Clark had left that province a weakened presence on the national stage. But what could the federal prime minister offer to the three "have" provinces that would convince them to back out of their social union demands, especially when he had no cards of personal loyalty to play? The answer was money. Alberta and Ontario, like all the provinces, were struggling to realign their health care systems. The federal government would soon be coming into billions of dollars of surplus. The *quid pro quo* was obvious: if the two richest provinces would accept a watered-down social union, Ottawa would increase transfers to them.

For months leading up to the 1999 budget, Harris had been demanding that the Canada Health and Social Transfer be increased and that the discriminatory caps incorporated into it be removed. Dianne Cunningham acknowledged that, in exchange for increased funding for health care, Ontario was prepared to modify its demands on the social union. It was vintage political horse-trading. The Liberals also calculated that increased funding to Ontario might solve another worrying problem. According to internal party polling, Ontario voters were becoming "disengaged" from the federal government. The Rae and Harris administrations, each in its own way, had brought home to voters just how important Queen's Park was to their lives: to their schools and hospitals, their daycare centres, and their local governments. Ottawa, meanwhile, was receding into the background as an increasingly irrelevant player that spent most of its time debating whether to buy some helicopters. If Ontario voters, the most federally minded in Canada, gave up on the federal government or, worse yet, came to agree with their provincial leaders that the economic deal of Confederation was no longer in their interest, the consequences for the federal government and the Liberal Party would be dire. Increasing funding to Ontario would remind voters that the federal government still counted.

The bitter price the Liberals would have to pay would be to provide Harris with desperately needed health money just as he went into an election. But they had no choice. "The last thing we wanted to do is to give him a gift that could help him get re-elected," Treasury Board president Marcel Massé told the Quebec MPs. "I hope we won't have to live with the re-election of Mike Harris." But "the resentment was becoming a threat to national unity ... When you are forced to make a political decision for the long-term benefit, you have to pay a price in the short term. [The probable re-election of Mike Harris] is one of them."[9]

The *quo* arrived with the *quid*. On February 4, 1999, fourteen days before Martin released his budget, which in total increased annual federal transfers to Ontario by $945 million, the federal government and the English Canadian provinces revealed their negotiated social union. (Quebec left the conference at the last minute, when it became clear that the other premiers were prepared to accept half a loaf in exchange for increased transfers.) The terms of the deal required the consent of a majority of the provincial governments before the federal government could launch any new program in areas of provincial jurisdiction, and promised a vaguely defined dispute-resolution mechanism in the event of a federal-provincial impasse. In exchange, Ontario and the other provinces gave up their demand for joint consultation in setting standards in health care, and a guarantee that Ottawa would never again slash transfers to provinces without their consent.

As he contemplated the tumult of the past four years, Jean Chrétien could be forgiven for believing that he had earned the right to a period of peace in provincial-federal relations. In response to the Quebec referendum and increased militancy from the "have" provinces, the federal government had given the major provinces vetoes over constitutional reform and had recognized legislatively the distinctness of Quebec society. The federal government had handed over a broad range of responsibilities to exclusive provincial jurisdiction and negotiated an accord with the English provinces to harmonize social policy. Finally, perhaps, after decades of failed and half-successful attempts to rebalance the Confederation, from the Rowell-Sirois Commission of 1940 to the Constitution Act, 1982, to the Meech Lake and Charlottetown accords, a new stability had finally been achieved, one that could see the country into the new millennium.

But it was not to be.

The federal Liberals might reasonably have hoped that Mike Harris's emphatic re-election victory in June 1999—the first back-to-back majority governments in Ontario since the days of John Robarts—would lead to an easing of tensions between the two capitals. After all, that victory had in part been purchased with health care money provided by Ottawa in its 1999 budget. Notwithstanding Allan Rock's angry vow to campaign against Harris's re-election, the Liberals stayed quiet during the election campaign, much to the chagrin of Ontario Liberal leader Dalton McGuinty. And, with a second government, Harris had affirmed the legitimacy of his Common Sense Revolution. He could afford to relax.

The opposite turned out to be true. While the Conservatives did slow down the pace of reform in their second mandate—compromising with doctors over primary care reform, negotiating with construction unions over labour law reform, and persuading the universities and community colleges by means of grants to reorient their focus to job training—relations with Ottawa went from worse to worse yet. Although Paul Martin, in his February 2000 budget, continued the trend towards restoring federal transfers to the provinces to 1980s levels, the Harris government launched a multimillion-dollar television campaign to convince voters that Ottawa was still not paying its fair share. And, in truth, despite the rising level of cash grants, the Canada Health and Social Transfer remained well below where it should have been. The reason was simple. With the federal books finally balanced, the Liberals were anxious to pass on some of the popular tax cuts that Ontario and other provinces had already delivered. There was limited room for Martin to cut taxes and increase transfers simultaneously. The Liberals soon discovered that the good news of their tax cuts had been overshadowed by the bad news about health care funding, as the provinces demanded a complete restoration of the transfers, no strings attached, and the Liberals hinted that the money might soon be coming, but with strings aplenty.

At first Allan Rock speculated grandly about a new national program in home care, primary care reform, and pharmacare. When the provinces, united, refused to consider any new program until funding had been restored, he beat a hasty retreat. By the time Chrétien met with the first ministers in September 2000, the federal shopping list had been reduced to a single, paltry item: in exchange for increased federal funding from $15.5 billion to $18.7 billion, the provinces would agree to submit report cards on how well they were delivering core health services, with the federal government influencing the terms of reference of the report cards. Lucien Bouchard rejected even this proposal, decrying it as a fresh federal intrusion into the provincial jurisdiction of health care. Mike Harris agreed. Two days before the summit began, he stood before the Ontario legislature with Bouchard and pledged that Ontario would not sign any deal that had not also been signed by Quebec. "It is not possible to have a deal without Quebec when it comes to health care for Canadians," he stated categorically.[10] The ultimatum angered even old allies like Ralph Klein, who was ready to sign and take the cheque. But Harris and Bouchard remained firm throughout the negotiations, which included a threat by Chrétien to deprive the two provinces of their share of the money if they walked away from the deal. In the end, Ottawa won nothing more than a seat at the table where the standards would be negotiated, based on its role as the provider of health services for Native people, veterans, and other recipients of direct federal funds. In other words, federal funding would increase, no strings attached. The Ontario-Quebec axis was alive and well, and once again flexing its considerable muscle.

But the Tories did not restrict themselves to the issue of health care alone. They fought Ottawa on myriad fronts: continued federal surpluses in Employment Insurance (which produced so much bad blood that the federal government signed deals to hand over responsibility for labour training to every province except Ontario); federal reluctance to toughen the Young Offenders' Act; the federal gun registry (Ontario opposed it as a bureaucratic waste of time and an infringement on the rights of gun owners); Ottawa's apparent willingness to agree at the Kyoto environmental negotiations to reducing greenhouse-gas levels so aggressively that Ontario's manufacturing base could be threatened; federal funding on infrastructure; and federal foot-dragging in creating the social union's dispute-resolution panel. Every day, it seemed, it was something else.

In part, the sound and fury stemmed from the Harris administration's own internal body clock. Harris and his advisers needed something to fight. They are brawlers by nature, whether it be with teachers, labour leaders, anti-poverty activists—anybody but doctors, who are bigger than they are. But in a larger sense the stresses between the two governments reflected the natural, if damaging, tensions within the federation, as Ontario drew farther and farther away from Ottawa and the rest of the country.

Finance Minister Eves also formally confirmed what had long been expected: that Ontario would detach itself from the federal income-tax system, effective January 1, 2001. While Ottawa would still define taxable income, collect it, and remit the tax to the provinces, Ontario would establish its own tax rates based directly on income, rather than as a percentage of the federal tax. All other provinces were following suit. In part, the decoupling resulted from federal moves to lower income taxes. Any provincial taxes linked directly to federal taxes would be forced down as well, and no provincial government wanted to grant its citizens a provincial income-tax cut without taking full credit for it. But the move also resulted from provincial frustration in getting Ottawa to let them tailor their taxes to individual needs, just as Eves had been frustrated by Ottawa's refusal to let Ontario impose its own Fair Share Health Care Levy. One year into the millennium, all ten provinces had individual income-tax regimes, with unknown implications for Ottawa's ability to manage a national tax policy.

Meanwhile, in Alberta, politically ambitious treasurer Stockwell Day had announced that his province would move to a flat tax, reversing almost a century's tradition of progressivity as the bedrock of the income-tax system. No longer would upper-income earners pay a higher rate of tax than middle- and lower-income earners. Everyone (with the exception of very low income earners) would pay a single rate of 11 per cent. Day took the flat tax notion with him when he captured the leadership of the new Canadian Alliance, successor to the Reform Party, in July 2000. Once again—as with the drive to balance budgets, cut taxes, and reform health care—the provinces were setting the agenda, with Ottawa struggling reluctantly to contain or catch up with the new initiative.

The trendline went only one way: towards schism.

CONCLUSION

The Next Ontario

Ontario's economy is the essence of its culture, and has been since the time of the first settlers. Various visionaries over the years have tried to construct a separate identity for Ontario, to turn it into a miniature replica of England, a reflection of American republicanism, the heartland of an economically and culturally independent Canada, a bastion of Protestant rectitude, an example of cooperative bilingualism, a community of multicultural communities. But any attempt to manufacture an identity for Ontario gets in the way of its true founding myth: this place was ordained by God, and realized through the efforts of its citizens, to grow. In the early days of a worldwide demand for wheat, it had the soil and the climate to make its first settlers prosperous farmers. It had the lumber, the iron ore, the nickel, the silver, and the gold to feed the industries sprouting up in the new towns that emerged across the province. It had the abundant waterfalls and swift-flowing rivers to harness the new electricity that turned factories into industrial giants.

It also had the rest of Canada. Thanks to Confederation, Ontario enjoyed guaranteed access to overseas markets through the St. Lawrence River. Thanks to the National Policy, it had high tariffs to protect new industries and compel consumers in other provinces to buy Ontario shirts and shoes, even though others would have cost less. Thanks to a compliant federal government, Ontario had guaranteed access to any natural resources it needed, from Sydney's coal to Alberta's oil, often at below-market rates. In exchange, the province magnanimously funded subsidies to the poorer regions (virtually the entire country), knowing that at least some of the money would come back in the form of purchased Ontario goods.

Finally, it had the United States, whose hardy settlers helped Ontario's population expand in the critical early years, and whose dynamism served as a model to copy—if not envy. U.S. capital helped Ontario industries modernize and expand after the Second World War. The managed trade pact in automobiles helped cement the province's industrial primacy in the 1960s and 1970s. And free trade guaranteed its now mature industries a market to compete in as the province prepared for the next millennium.

It is tempting at times to despair of Ontario's obsession with growth and wealth. Its cities burgeon, chewing up the countryside and absorbing fine old towns into homogenous suburbs. Attempts at fostering a unique indigenous culture (which, unfortunately, no one has been able to define) are overwhelmed by Hollywood and the Internet. Efforts to preserve the Ontarian and Canadian welfare state—a unique amalgam of European and American precedents—are being undermined by factory workers who prefer tax cuts to safety nets, and who vote massively for Mike Harris even as their union dues are used by labour leaders in futile attempts at defeating him.

But those who love to hate Ontario simply fail, or refuse, to consider its astonishing strengths. Ontario is a cultural dynamo no arts council could ever imagine, let alone create—the national centre of publishing, music, the visual arts, and the media. It is one of the world's most tolerant places, as each new influx of immigrants—the old stock Loyalists and Brits, Irish Catholics, Germans, eastern and southern Europeans, and the latest waves from the Caribbean and Asia—sweeps away succeeding generations of intolerance and privilege. This province of perpetual pioneers has dispatched old boy networks into the hands of bankruptcy trustees, turned our downtowns into year-long expositions of international cuisine, and made our university campuses the ultimate melting pots. Has any community anywhere in the world accepted so many different kinds of people and absorbed them so harmoniously? Is there another city in the world culturally more diverse than Toronto? Has any society anywhere enjoyed such an unbroken history of peace, personal liberty, and intellectual and material progress? Are not these the hallmarks of a flourishing civilization?

Yes, Ontario is self-interested, and always has been. If Ontarians historically have been willing to give more than they got, through subsidies to other parts of Canada, the compensations extended beyond the warmth that comes from doing good. Ontario's transfers helped cement east-west trade, protected its industries from outside competition, secured needed natural resources, and made its customers dependants. Equalization payments were simply worthwhile investments in preserving a union that was, at the end, to Ontario's advantage. But if other regions have chafed at relying on handouts from Ontario, even as it keeps them under its economic thumb, none has, as yet, been prepared to repudiate the arrangement.

If Ontario historically has suffered from any fault, it is complacency, a certain expectation of unending prosperity and—within Canada at least—supremacy. Even in the Depression, Ontarians knew that times were not as bad for them as they were for most others. Hubris can be a sign of a civilization in decline. During the last quarter of the twentieth century, Ontario had its cozy protective blanket stripped away by oil shocks, bad government, NAFTA, GATT, and the emergence of an unforgiving global market. But, in the end, the province adjusted, even thrived, discarding its low-value branch plants for aggressive, export-oriented high-technology firms. While certain backward-looking political economists continue to describe Canadians as hewers of wood and drawers of water, Ontario builds what is emerging as

North America's most advanced bio-technology industry and steadily expands its communications sector. The province is successfully adjusting to the challenges of the twenty-first century.

But as Ontario and the other regions of the country shift away from the east-west to the north-south or the overseas axis, the federation's reason for being, as we know it, is gradually dissolving. Ontario's relations with the rest of the country are being transformed, almost by the month. Some might call it a change in the Canadian culture; others might point to the transformation of the Canadian economy. The point, as far as Ontario is concerned, is moot: What matters is that Ontario is increasingly going it alone. In 1998, for example, Michigan governor John Engler revised his state's business taxes, resulting in a new proposed levy on out-of-state businesses. The Ontario government acted with alarm: the new tax would cost Ontario companies trading into Michigan millions of dollars, jeopardizing the $50 billion trade relationship between the province and the state. After urgent negotiations involving Ottawa, Toronto, and Lansing, Engler agreed to revise the tax, largely exempting Ontario firms. This near-miss convinced senior bureaucrats in both Michigan and Ontario that the Great Lakes provinces and states would eventually have to sign their own agreement not to impose non-tariff barriers on each other's goods. The agreement would not be binding in law, since only the American and Canadian federal governments can sign treaties, but it would signal the next step down the road to Ontario's integration into a larger North American economy.

The federal government has been both the instigator and the victim of Ontario's gradual devolution. First, as it retreated through the 1980s and 1990s from the social policy field, Ottawa's influence over both the economy and society shrivelled, exposing the provincial governments as the prime players in shaping health care, education, welfare, housing, and other social services. Then, with its participation in the GATT, the World Trade Organization, and

NAFTA, the federal government further circumscribed its ability to exert force by manipulating tariffs. The world of free trade is the world of smaller government, for better or for worse.

All these developments were bound to downsize Ottawa's importance to Ontario, in particular, as changing circumstances encouraged the province to pursue a separate destiny within a North American economic community. But Parliament Hill's position has become ever more exposed. Bereft of any real economic power, and increasingly limited in its ability to influence social policy, the federal government has become essentially an agent of redistribution, siphoning funds from the wealthy regions of Canada—principally Ontario—and distributing the money to poorer regions. These redistributions made some sense when they helped preserve the east-west economy, but now that this economy is vanishing, they increasingly become transfers that infringe on Ontario's self-interest. The Chrétien government is not insensitive to the issue, which is why, in 1999, it removed the discriminatory caps that had been placed on transfers to Ontario, and, in 2000, negotiated a new health agreement that restored federal payments to levels not seen in a decade. But the principle remains: to the extent that Ottawa takes money from Ontario and gives it to the rest of the country, with no concomitant benefit to the province, it risks alienating Ontarians.

This conflict places any government in Ottawa in an intolerable contradiction. Winning Ontario is essential to forming a federal government. The current Liberal administration relies on Ontario for 100 of its 172 seats. If the Liberal Party were to lose Ontario's support, it would collapse. Yet how can it expect to retain that support if the deal that it offers Ontario's citizens is not in their interest? The conundrum is unresolvable. The administration relies on the votes and revenues of one region, which it then bleeds on behalf of the other regions. Given that one of the receiving regions, Quebec, is in a perpetual state of near revolt through dissatisfactions of its own, the situation for Canada as we now know it becomes increasingly bleak.

Ottawa has been challenged by autonomy-seeking provinces before. As we have seen, Ontario has been its bane through much of Confederation. But outside forces served to boost the powers of the federal government at critical periods in our history. By far the most important was war. The First World War reversed the trend towards increasing provincial autonomy, allowing Ottawa to temporarily gather all the reins of government into its own hands and to launch the income tax, a source of revenue it would dominate from then on. The Second World War enlarged Ottawa's powers even more, making it virtually the sole financier of Confederation. And the postwar legacy of the modern industrial welfare state expanded Ottawa's powers once again, turning even Ontario into a virtual vassal of the central power.

But Canada has not been formally at war for more than fifty years. Our armed forces, once a major source of expenditure and an agent for internal economic development, are a wraith of their former selves. Without the centralizing tendency of war, the federal government finds its powers slowly dissipating. No wonder Ottawa proudly trumpets its peacekeeping missions, eagerly sends troops to plough Toronto's snowy streets, and appears to tolerate endless scandals and alarms in the military. At least it reminds people the army still exists.

There appears to be little doubt that the world has moved away from tariffs, subsidies, incentives, and the other tools of industrial policy beloved by nation-states. These changes leave states with little to do, especially federal states, which have less to do than others. And, with Canada one of the weakest federal states, Ottawa is left with the least. Its surviving areas of competence are meagre indeed. Canals, airports, and harbours are now either redundant or locally managed. Telecommunications are escaping the regulatory grasp of the federal power, dissipating over the Internet and other emerging technologies. Ottawa determines immigration levels, but

Ontario is now responsible for settling and caring for the majority of this country's immigrants, with Quebec and British Columbia in charge of most of the rest. Embassies mean less today than they once did, now that cell phones, computers, and bank cards make it easy for citizens to navigate the world without the help of their host state.

Ottawa still manages the money supply, although that function has been almost entirely delegated to the governor of the Bank of Canada. It makes criminal law. It exerts influence over the lives of Canadians through direct transfers: Employment Insurance, the Canada Pension Plan, and old age security. But these plans are largely self-managing, and, in Ontario's case, they often serve only to further exacerbate the inequities of the federation, especially through the imbalance in Employment Insurance premiums. In short, there is little left to keep the federal government busy. And when it tries to find work, the result often provokes the government of Ontario.

Does this mean that Ontario will, out of economic self-interest, eventually disengage entirely from the rest of Canada? Not necessarily.

There are several possible tomorrows for the province, for the other regions of the country, and for Canada itself. While the flow of history can sometimes be discerned, the chronicle of a people is one of accidents as much as imperatives. Had 30,000 people who voted No in the 1995 referendum voted Yes, we would be living in a very different country today, and might not be living in one called Canada at all. Ontario's destiny is as dependent on Quebec's, on the United States', and on the world's as it is on its own exertions. And, as we have watched throughout our history, the quality and character of leaders, and how they react to each other, can do much to shape the course of events.

The federal government retains one, and perhaps only one, potent defence against the rising tide of provincial power: the disunity of the federal conservative alternative to the governing Liberals. In the 1993 election the Progressive Conservative Party entered into a long, slow, and—as yet—unchecked decline, while the new populist and libertarian Reform Party captured conservative support in the West. Ontario right-wing voters found themselves divided between Tory and Reform sympathies. They split the vote, ensuring Liberal victories in almost every riding and a Liberal government in Ottawa.

Following the 1997 election, in which the Ontario right once again proved that a house divided cannot stand against united Liberals, Reform attempted to woo both disaffected federal conservatives and the non-aligned Ontario Progressive Conservative Party of Mike Harris. But even with a new name (the Canadian Alliance), a new leader (former Alberta treasurer Stockwell Day), and new policies, including a proposed flat income tax, the Alliance failed to heal the conservative rift in Ontario. In the November 2000 election, which Chrétien called prematurely to exploit the Alliance's disorganization, the Liberals effectively exposed the former Pentecostal preacher's dogmatic evangelical Christianity, his inexperience on the national stage, and voter disquiet over proposed reforms that would have permitted citizens to force referendums on abortion and other contentious topics. Although the Reform/Alliance vote in Ontario improved from 19 to 24 per cent, and the party secured a toenail-hold of two seats in the Ottawa Valley, the Liberals retained 100 of the 103 seats, enough to assure yet another comfortable majority government for the prime minister.

But the right in Canada cannot forever remain in schism. Eventually, the Alliance, alone or in conjunction with the Progressive Conservatives, will take power and the political map of Canada will be transformed. For the Alliance espouses three principles that have been essential demands of recent Ontario governments. First, transfers from Ontario, Alberta, and (on a good day) British Columbia to the rest of the country must cease, beyond the agreed equalization payments. There must be no more covert draining of dollars from haves to have-nots through economic development programs, EI training schemes, or other back-channel devices. Second, the Alliance is committed to reducing the federal government's role in social policy, restoring to the provinces the right and responsibility for funding and delivering health care, education, municipal works, public housing, and other domestic responsibilities. Third, the Alliance's determination to cut federal spending overall, both for its own sake and to finance further tax cuts, will diminish the role and relevance of the federal government even more. The federation, under the Alliance, would become what observers have long predicted it must become anyway and what Oliver Mowat fought for more than a century ago: a collection of autonomous regions, joined in a monetary and customs union, with a weak federal authority coordinating that union and representing it before the rest of the world.

Regardless of the Alliance's electoral future, however, such changes are likely, perhaps inevitable. The question is simply one of degree and time. As we have seen, the Ontario government and people care most about preserving the resources, capital, and access to markets on which their prosperity depends, and will act accordingly. To the extent that the federal government protects and enhances this new status quo, by expanding the free trade zone through negotiations to include other states in Latin America, say, or by lowering federal taxes to increase competitiveness, Ontario will welcome its assistance. To the extent that it obstructs the smooth operation of Ontario's economic machine, by siphoning off wealth for redistribution, by spending on programs Ontarians don't feel they need or would rather provide out of their own resources, or by engaging in fiscal or economic policies that damage Ontario's competitiveness, the province will resist. With Ontario stronger and more autonomous than at any time since Confederation, and with Ottawa weaker, that resistance could prove fatal to the union.

Others across Canada may marvel at the insolence of such an analysis. For more than 130 years they have chafed at the domination of central Canada. To them, ever since Confederation, Ontario has siphoned off the nation's natural resources and forced others to buy them back as finished goods at artificially high prices. Similarly, the hated Bay Street starved regional enterprises of capital and offered the rest of Canada nothing in return but a few grudging dollars in federal loans and grants. Now, at the very instant when the central-Canadian bankers and bureaucrats conclude that the relationship no longer works to Ontario's advantage, they demand a different deal.

All this is absolutely true. It is also, of course, the way of the world. But the new world, and the new arrangements in Confederation it will force, stand to benefit the rest of Canada as much as Ontario. The same north-south and global pulls that have reshaped the Ontario economy offer similar opportunities elsewhere. New Brunswick, as its provincial leadership has been increasingly aggressive in asserting, boasts a highly skilled and bilingual labour force with lower wage rates than most Canadian and American markets. And, in today's economy, a computer can work from anywhere. Already Atlantic Canadian economists and politicians are probing the European market, quietly talking up the shared history and values of the North Atlantic community. The European island communities—especially Iceland and the Isle of Man—are now in regular contact with Newfoundland and Prince Edward Island, exploring possible economic and trading links. Iceland Air recently inaugurated a service linking Halifax to European capitals via Reykjavik. The possibilities are endless. They are certainly more promising than the traditional debilitating dependence on federal subsidies and supports for chronically underemployed workers in declining industries—many of which, especially fishing, the federal government has helped to destroy.

It is possible to envision a new Canada in the twenty-first century, a true confederation of autonomous regions, each thriving in its own unique circumstances, bound by a shared history and values, linked through a federal agency that represents these regions' common interests to each other and to the rest of the world, and with the regions conferring on shared policies and principles in matters of their own jurisdiction. It is a Canada we're already halfway towards. Some will mourn its loss of unity and common purpose; others will celebrate its diversity and the independence of each family within its own house. Can our long-cherished commitment to national standards in social policy endure under such centrifugal forces? Yes, and they can be strengthened too. When the Ontario government in 1996 embarked on a new and tougher curriculum for its elementary and secondary schools, it discovered that the western provinces and the Atlantic provinces had each launched joint curriculum projects (the Western and Atlantic common curriculums) and were in regular communication with each other. Ontario borrowed heavily from both initiatives, creating for the first time in the nation's history something resembling a common curriculum throughout English Canada. The likelihood is greater than ever before that a family moving from Burnaby, BC, to Truro, NS, will find their new local school teaching their children similar lessons in similar grades—a major and convenient unifying cultural force. Can anyone imagine the fractiousness that would have ensued had the federal government attempted to negotiate a national common curriculum from the top down? National standards are best defined and preserved as joint agreements among provinces, not as federal dictums.

It is also entirely possible, of course, that Canada will be lost. That decision will be up to Quebec, and then Ontario, and finally the West. The surprise decision in January 2001 by Lucien Bouchard to step down as premier increased the possibility both of another referendum on separation, sooner rather than later, and of the Parti Québécois' defeat in the next provincial election. But whether provincial Liberals or the PQ are in power, Quebec's agenda remains essentially the same, for all Quebec premiers are nationalist, and all seek to protect its internal sovereignty against federalist incursions. If Quebec ever should evolve or launch itself toward sovereignty, in which it assumes effective unilateral control over everything happening within its own borders, Ontario will quickly follow suit. Canada without Quebec is impossible. In such a Canada, Ontario would represent 50 per cent of its population and about 55 per cent of its gross domestic product, and could have an absolute majority of seats in the House of Commons. It would overwhelm the federation. The West, in particular, would want a separate destiny from one attached to such a giant, and Ontario would have no interest in providing succour to the poorer remnants of the federation. More important, Ontario would certainly not permit the federal government to negotiate the terms of Quebec's departure from Confederation in the event of a Yes vote, despite the seeming insistence of the federal government under the 2000 "clarity" legislation that the provinces can only endorse, rather than participate in, such negotiations. Ontario has compelling bilateral relations with Quebec: they share the Great Lakes–St. Lawrence Seaway, and the provinces enjoy the most important interprovincial trade relationship in the country, even if that relationship, in both cases, is dwarfed by trade with the United States. Any responsible Ontario government would move quickly, in the event of the clear and present danger of Quebec separation, to secure bilateral trade and transportation arrangements with the emerging nation. Before anything else, the two economies would seek to protect themselves by protecting each other from the shocks of separation. The rest would be mere paperwork. That paperwork, if circumstances dictated, might even involve a declaration of Ontario's sovereignty.

There are other possibilities as well. The northern and northwestern expanses of Ontario have long felt themselves alienated from and exploited by the south. There is no doubt that urban southern Ontario has treated rural northern Ontario as a quasi-colonial possession, exploiting its natural wealth while subsidizing its dispersed population. Northern Ontario is also home to much of the province's Indian population, with many land claims still to be settled. The First Nations have already declared that they would not recognize any unilateral declaration of sovereignty by Quebec; one can imagine how they would react to any similar move by Ontario. And, as numerous political scientists and economists have observed, the world's nation-state and sub-state borders may be breaking down everywhere as a new civilizational order based on city-states emerges. Much has been made of the "Four Motors of Europe"—the regions of Rhone-Alps (Lyon) in France, Catalonia (Barcelona) in Spain, Lombardy (Milan) in Italy, and Baden Württemberg (Stuttgart) in Germany—which communicate directly with each other and with the European Union government, as well as with their national governments. Perhaps the same is happening here, and the Ontario we have talked about throughout this book is, in truth, simply the economic nexus of the province, the Toronto-London-St. Catharines conurbation, a region that interacts with other regions—Detroit, Montreal, Chicago—as much as with any state, provincial, or national government.

The destination is uncertain; only the direction of travel appears clear.

One hundred years ago, the geo-political world was vastly different from today. Much of it was composed of authoritarian empires: the Hapsburgs dominating central Europe, the Romanovs reigning in Russia, the Ottomans astride the Bosporus, and the Hohenzollerns galvanizing Germany. What today we call the Third World was a colonial hodge-podge, under the sway of Great Britain and lesser imperial powers. The United States was an isolationist bastion, protected by two oceans and determined to pursue its manifest destiny to dominate North America, while leaving the rest of the world to itself. Canada was an autonomous dominion within the British Empire, not yet in control of its foreign policy, and its industries still subservient to agriculture. Fifty years later the empires were gone, the tsars and emperors largely deposed after two calamitous world wars, the decolonized Third World struggling to take control of its own destiny, and the world in the thrall of two blocs locked in mortal, if mostly non-violent, combat, with the Soviet Union tightly controlling one and the United States the other. Today, all of that is gone as well, as the world reverts to its original gaggle of civilizations, with the United States, the last empire, trying with mixed success to keep the peace, and Canada ever more integrated into its sphere.

If things have changed so much, and so many times, in one hundred years, what awaits us in the next fifty? Are there children being born today who will live in a Canada of regional states rather than provinces? Will the world still be one of economic blocs, and how many and how powerful will they be? Will the industrialized world have gone through a century and a half without a major war, and what effect will such a prolonged peace have on the progress of our separate and collective civilizations?

These are hopeful questions. Canada and the world are not flying apart. We are growing towards future relationships we cannot yet fully envision, but have no reason to fear. We have every reason to hope they will evolve peacefully and to the benefit of all.

But whatever future awaits us, Canada's central province will pursue its destiny aggressively and with confidence. As it always has.

Notes

Introduction: Accounting for Ontario

1 "Harris threatens to sue Ottawa," *Globe and Mail*, May 5, 1998, A10.

2 Ibid.

1: "Some Joint Authority"

1 G.P. deT. Glazebrook, *Life in Ontario: A Social History* (Toronto: University of Toronto Press, 1968), 35.

2 *Globe*, January 22, 1863, quoted in S.J.R. Noel, *Patrons, Clients, Brokers: Ontario Society and Politics, 1791–1896* (Toronto: University of Toronto Press, 1990), 201.

3 J.M.S. Careless, *Brown of the Globe*, vol. 1: *The Voice of Upper Canada, 1818–1859* (Toronto: Macmillan, 1959), 315.

4 Ibid., 317.

5 Ibid., 321.

6 Ibid.

7 Ibid.

8 Ibid., 322.

2: Macdonald's Bane

1 J.M.S. Careless, *Brown of the Globe*, vol. 2: *Statesman of Confederation, 1860–1880* (Toronto: Macmillan, 1963), 120.

2 Ibid., 128.

3 Christopher Moore, *1867: How the Fathers Made a Deal* (Toronto: McClelland & Stewart, 1997), 51.

4 Ibid., 58.

5 Careless, *Brown of the Globe*, 2: 165–66.

6 Moore, *1867: How the Fathers Made a Deal*, 55.

7 Christopher Armstrong, *The Politics of Federalism: Ontario's Relations with the Federal Government, 1867–1942* (Toronto: University of Toronto Press, 1981), 11.

8 Careless, *Brown of the Globe*, 2: 171.

9 A. Margaret Evans, *Sir Oliver Mowat* (Toronto: University of Toronto Press, 1992), 10.

10 Moore, *1867: How the Fathers Made a Deal*, 124.

11 Noel, *Patrons, Clients, Brokers: Ontario Society and Politics, 1791–1896* (Toronto: University of Toronto Press, 1990), 220.

12 Armstrong, *The Politics of Federalism*, 11.

13 Noel, *Patrons, Clients, Brokers*, 264.

14 Armstrong, *The Politics of Federalism*, 13.

15 Ibid., 14.

16 Evans, *Sir Oliver Mowat*, 162.

17 Ibid., 147.

18 Ibid., 14.

19 Ibid., 157.

20 Ibid., 154.

21 Armstrong, *The Politics of Federalism*, 21.

22 Evans, *Sir Oliver Mowat*, 161.

23 Noel, *Patrons, Clients, Brokers*, 257.

24 This particular argument was made before the Supreme Court of Canada, which sided with the federal government. Evans, *Sir Oliver Mowat*, 155.

25 Ibid., 173.

26 Noel, *Patrons, Clients, Brokers*, 260.

27 Robert Bothwell, *A Short History of Ontario* (Edmonton: Hurtig, 1986), 85.

28 Armstrong, *The Politics of Federalism*, 61.

3: Ottawa Wins at War

1 Royce MacGillivray, *The Mind of Ontario* (Belleville: Mika Publishing, 1985), 93.

2 Christopher Armstrong, *The Politics of Federalism: Ontario's Relations with the Federal Government, 1867–1942* (Toronto: University of Toronto Press, 1981), 28.

3 Ibid., 60.

4 David R. Cameron, "Post-Modern Ontario and the Laurentian Thesis," in Douglas Brown and Janet Hiebert, eds., *Canada: The State of the Federation, 1994* (Kingston: Institute of Intergovernmental Relations, 1994), 111.

5 Michael Bliss, *Right Honourable Men: The Descent of Canadian Politics from Macdonald to Mulroney* (Toronto: HarperCollins, 1994), 77–78.

6 Neil McKenty, *Mitch Hepburn* (Toronto: McClelland & Stewart, 1967), 72.

7 Robert Bothwell, *A Short History of Ontario* (Edmonton: Hurtig, 1986), 139.

8 McKenty, *Mitch Hepburn*, 253.

9 Ibid., 160–61.

10 Ibid., 228–29.

4: "Does Ontario Exist?"

1 Randall White, *Ontario, 1610–1985* (Toronto: Dundurn, 1985), 269.

2 Marc Gotlieb, "George Drew and the Dominion-Provincial Conference on Reconstruction of 1945–6," in Michael Piva, ed., *A History of Ontario: Selected Readings* (Toronto: Copp Clark Pitman, 1988), 247.

3 Ibid., 251.

4 Ibid., 253.

5 Roger Graham, *Old Man Ontario: Leslie M. Frost* (Toronto: University of Toronto Press, 1990), 126.

6 Ibid., 123.

7 Ibid., 155.

8 Jonathan Manthorpe, *The Power and the Tories: Ontario Politics—1943 to the Present* (Toronto: Macmillan, 1974), 41.

9 Quoted in White, *Ontario*, 276.

10 Ibid., 278.

11 Manthorpe, *The Power and the Tories*, 58.

12 A.K. McDougall, *John P. Robarts: His Life and Government* (Toronto: University of Toronto Press, 1986), 132.

13 Ibid., 212.

14 David R. Cameron, "Post-Modern Ontario and the Laurentian Thesis," in Douglas Brown and Janet Hiebert, eds., *Canada: The State of the Federation, 1994* (Kingston: Institute of Intergovernmental Relations, 1994), 111.

15 Keith G. Banting, "The Past Speaks to the Future: Lessons from the Postwar Social Union," in Harvey Lazar, ed., *Canada: The State of the Federation, 1997: Non-Constitutional Renewal* (Kingston: Institute of Intergovernmental Relations, 1997), 53.

16 Royce MacGillivray, *The Mind of Ontario* (Belleville: Mika Publishing, 1985), 88.

17 White, *Ontario*, 292.

18 David Milne, *Tug of War: Ottawa and the Provinces under Trudeau and Mulroney* (Toronto: James Lorimer, 1986), 70.

19 Thomas Courchene with Colin Telmer, *From Heartland to North American Region State: The Social, Fiscal and Federal Evolution of Ontario* (Toronto: Faculty of Management, University of Toronto, 1998), 60.

20 Ibid., 61.

21 Milne, *Tug of War*, 15.

5: Failures and Betrayals

1 Desmond Morton, "*Sic Permanet*: Ontario People and Their Politics," in Graham White, ed., *The Government and Politics of Ontario*, 4th ed. (Toronto: Nelson, 1990), 6.

2 Georgette Gagnon and Dan Rath, *Not Without Cause: David Peterson's Fall from Grace* (Toronto: HarperCollins, 1991), 43.

3 Ibid., 44.

4 Thomas Courchene with Colin Telmer, *From Heartland to North American Region State: The Social, Fiscal and Federal Evolution of Ontario* (Toronto: Faculty of Management, University of Toronto, 1998), 62.

5 H.V. Nelles, "'Red Tied': *Fin de Siècle* Politics in Ontario," in Michael S. Whittington and Glen Williams, eds., *Canadian Politics in the 1990s*, 3rd ed. (Toronto: Nelson Canada, 1990), 76.

6 Gagnon and Rath, *Not Without Cause*, 173.

7 Jonathan Manthorpe, *The Power and the Tories: Ontario Politics—1943 to the Present* (Toronto: Macmillan, 1974), 179.

8 S.F. Wise, "The Ontario Political Culture: A Study in Complexities," in Graham White, ed., *The Government and Politics of Ontario*, 4th ed. (Toronto: Nelson, 1990), 48.

9 Gagnon and Rath, *Not Without Cause*, 158.

10 Ibid., 145.

11 George Ehring and Wayne Roberts, *Giving Away a Miracle: Lost Dreams and Broken Promises and the Ontario NDP* (Oakville: Mosaic Press, 1993), 286.

12 Bob Rae, *From Protest to Power: Personal Reflections on a Life in Politics* (Toronto: Viking, 1996), 174.

13 Thomas J. Courchene, *What Does Ontario Want? The 1988 Robarts Lecture* (North York: York University, 1989), 40.

14 Ibid., 25.

15 Ibid., 46.

16 Donald W. Stevenson, "Ontario and Confederation: A Reassessment," in Ronald L. Watts and Douglas M. Brown, eds., *Canada: The State of the Federation 1989* (Kingston: Institute of Intergovernmental Relations, 1989), 67.

17 Nelles, "'Red Tied,'" 76.

18 Rae, *From Protest to Power*, 178.

19 Ibid., 175.

20 Ibid., 190.

21 Thomas Walkom, *Rae Days* (Toronto: Key Porter Books, 1994), 98.

22 Rae, *From Protest to Power*, 201.

23 Courchene with Telmer, *From Heartland to North American Region State*, 149.

24 Government of Ontario, *Ontarians Expect Fairness from the Federal Government* (Toronto, 1995), 10.

6: Mowat's Heir

1 John Ibbitson, *Promised Land: Inside the Mike Harris Revolution* (Toronto: Prentice Hall, 1997), 48.

2 Ibid., 147.

3 "Martin enters fray over tax cut promise," *Toronto Star*, May 13, 1995, A10.

4 Edward Greenspon and Anthony Wilson-Smith, *Double Vision: The Inside Story of the Liberals in Power* (Toronto: Doubleday, 1996), 338.

5 "Deal to replace GST evades Ottawa," *Globe and Mail*, April 2, 1996, A10.

6 "PM firm on national medicare standards," ibid., August 25, 1998, A7.

7 "Harris threatens to sue Ottawa," ibid., May 2, 1998, A10.

8 "Harris is history, Rock predicts," *Ottawa Citizen*, October 2, 1998, A1.

9 "Transfers will help re-elect Mike Harris, Liberals admit," *National Post*, February 18, 1999, A1.

10 "Alliance of Quebec, Ontario is reborn," *Globe and Mail*, September 9, 2000, A5.

Acknowledgements

1 "Ontario ripe for 'separatism': Heartland shifting to 'region state,' economist says," *Ottawa Citizen*, January 17, 1998, A1.

2 Statistics were compiled from Ontario and federal government sources, or from works that cited these sources.

Bibliography

Armstrong, Christopher. *The Politics of Federalism: Ontario's Relations with the Federal Government, 1867–1942*. Toronto: University of Toronto Press, 1981

Banting, Keith G. "The Past Speaks to the Future: Lessons from the Postwar Social Union," in Harvey Lazar, ed., *Canada: The State of the Federation, 1997: Non-Constitutional Renewal*. Kingston: Institute of Intergovernmental Relations, 1997

Bliss, Michael. *Right Honourable Men: The Descent of Canadian Politics from Macdonald to Mulroney*. Toronto: HarperCollins, 1994

Bothwell, Robert. *A Short History of Ontario*. Edmonton: Hurtig, 1986

Cameron, David R. "Post-Modern Ontario and the Laurentian Thesis," in Douglas M. Brown and Janet Hiebert, eds., *Canada: The State of the Federation, 1994*. Kingston: Institute of Intergovernmental Relations, 1994

Careless, J.M.S. *Brown of The Globe*, 2 vols. Toronto: Macmillan, 1959 and 1963

Courchene, Thomas. *ACCESS: A Convention on the Canadian Economic and Social Systems*. Government of Ontario, Ministry of Intergovernmental Affairs, 1996. Unpublished

Courchene, Thomas J. *What Does Ontario Want? The 1988 Robarts Lecture*. North York: York University, 1989

Courchene, Thomas J., with Colin R. Telmer. *From Heartland to North*

American Region State: The Social, Fiscal and Federal Evolution of Ontario. Toronto: Faculty of Management, University of Toronto, 1998

Ehring, George, and Wayne Roberts. *Giving Away a Miracle: Lost Dreams and Broken Promises and the Ontario NDP*. Oakville: Mosaic Press, 1993

Evans, A. Margaret. *Sir Oliver Mowat*. Toronto: University of Toronto Press, 1992

Gagnon, Georgette, and Dan Rath. *Not Without Cause: David Peterson's Fall from Grace*. Toronto: HarperCollins, 1991

Glazebrook, G.P. deT. *Life in Ontario: A Social History*. Toronto: University of Toronto Press, 1968

Gotlieb, Marc J. "George Drew and the Dominion-Provincial Conference on Reconstruction of 1945–6," in Michael J. Piva, ed., *A History of Ontario: Selected Readings*. Toronto: Copp Clark Pitman, 1988

Government of Ontario. *Ontarians Expect Fairness from the Federal Government*. Toronto, 1995

Graham, Roger. *Old Man Ontario: Leslie M. Frost*. Toronto: University of Toronto Press, 1990

Greenspon, Edward, and Anthony Wilson-Smith. *Double Vision: The Inside Story of the Liberals in Power*. Toronto: Doubleday, 1996

Harney, Robert F., and Harold Troper. *Immigrants: A Portrait of the Urban Experience, 1890–1930*. Toronto: Van Nostrand Reinhold, 1975

Hoy, Claire. *Bill Davis*. Toronto: Methuen, 1985

Ibbitson, John. *Promised Land: Inside the Mike Harris Revolution*. Toronto: Prentice Hall, 1997

Loyal She Remains: A Pictorial History of Ontario. Toronto: United Empire Loyalists Association of Canada, 1984

Macdonald, Donald C., ed. *The Government and Politics of Ontario*. Toronto: Macmillan, 1975; rev. ed., Van Nostrand Reinhold, 1980; 3rd ed., Nelson, 1985

MacGillivray, Royce. *The Mind of Ontario*. Belleville: Mika Publishing, 1985

Manthorpe, Jonathan. *The Power and the Tories: Ontario Politics—1943 to the Present*. Toronto: Macmillan, 1974

McCallum, John. *Unequal Beginnings: Agriculture and Economic Development in Quebec and Ontario until 1870*. Toronto: University of Toronto Press, 1980

McDougall, A.K. *John P. Robarts: His Life and Government*. Toronto: University of Toronto Press, 1986

McKenty, Neil. *Mitch Hepburn*. Toronto: McClelland & Stewart, 1967

Milne, David. *Tug of War: Ottawa and the Provinces under Trudeau and Mulroney*. Toronto: James Lorimer, 1986

Moore, Christopher. *1867: How the Fathers Made a Deal*. Toronto: McClelland & Stewart, 1997

Nelles, H.V. "'Red Tied': *Fin de Siècle* Politics in Ontario," in Michael S. Whittington and Glen Williams, eds., *Canadian Politics in the 1990s*, 3rd ed. Toronto: Nelson, 1990

Noel, S.J.R. *Patrons, Clients, Brokers: Ontario Society and Politics, 1791–1896*. Toronto: University of Toronto Press, 1990

Rae, Bob. *From Protest to Power: Personal Reflections on a Life in Politics*. Toronto: Viking, 1996

Riendeau, Roger E. *Mississauga: An Illustrated History*. Northridge, CA: Windsor Publications, 1985

Robarts, John P. *Ontario in Confederation*. Toronto: Government of Ontario, 1968

Stevenson, Donald W. "Ontario and Confederation: A Reassessment," in Ronald L. Watts and Douglas M. Brown, eds., *Canada: The State of the Federation, 1989*. Kingston: Institute of Intergovernmental Relations, 1989

Walkom, Thomas. *Rae Days*. Toronto: Key Porter Books, 1994

White, Graham., ed. *The Government and Politics of Ontario*, 4th ed. Toronto: Nelson, 1990; 5th ed., University of Toronto Press, 1997

White, Randall. *Ontario, 1610–1985*. Toronto: Dundurn, 1985

White, Randall. *Ontario since 1985*. Toronto: eastendbooks, 1998

Acknowledgements

Early in 1998, Thomas Courchene and Colin Telmer published a small book, *From Heartland to North American Region State: The Social, Fiscal and Federal Evolution of Ontario*. Within days of publication, word of its content had raced through the precincts of Queen's Park; it was harder to get a copy than to get a straight answer out of Health Minister Elizabeth Witmer. Courchene and Telmer set out, in stark and uncompromising language, the economic disadvantage of Confederation to Ontario. The province, predicted the authors, was evolving from the glue that bound Canada together into an autonomous region state within the American/Canadian Great Lakes region, with possibly dire consequences for the federal government. When asked his opinion of the book, historian Michael Bliss declared that Courchene "is almost a nascent Ontario separatist. And my problem with that is [that] I'm a Canadian."[1]

I was fascinated by the contradiction between Courchene's thesis, which crystallized many of my own much more incoherent musings on the battles raging between the Harris and Chrétien governments, and Michael Bliss's rejoinder. The idea of Ontario separatism was nonsensical, yet something profound was happening to the province, something Courchene and Telmer had unearthed in *Heartland*. Others recognized its importance as well: the book became the subject of academic symposiums and was awarded the first Donner Prize for a work on public policy.

The answer to the paradox of an Ontario, devoid of separatist sentiment, that was nonetheless spinning out of Confederation might lie in the province's history, Phyllis Bruce suggested over a drink one autumn afternoon in 1999. We were discussing whether I should write a book under her HarperCollins imprint. There had been few good chronicles of this large but ambiguous province, she said. I don't recall which one of us came up with the idea of a book to place the heightening conflict between Queen's Park and Parliament Hill within the context of Ontario's political history and its future as predicted by Professor Courchene. I do remember that the title of the book emerged out of thin air within a matter of minutes, and that we excitedly jotted down chapter headings on cocktail napkins, just as in the movies.

As I began researching the political contests that forged Ontario—responsible government, Confederation, the war between Premier Oliver Mowat and Prime Minister John A. Macdonald, the struggles over electricity and taxation, the more recent conflicts concerning free trade and federal transfers—it became clear that the duel between the present provincial and federal governments was part of a historical and philosophical struggle to define the powers and limits of the two governments, a struggle that had confronted Ontario since before Confederation. *Unequal Beginnings: Agriculture and Economic Development in Quebec and Ontario until 1870*, John McCallum's history of Ontario's early successes in growing wheat, helped anchor my thesis about the links between Ontario's colonial economy and its imperialist state of mind. Early Ontario's political imbroglios were superbly chronicled by Sid Noel in *Patrons, Clients, Brokers: Ontario Society and Politics, 1791–1896*, and J.M.S. Careless's two-volume *Brown of the Globe* was invaluable. For the debate over Confederation itself I relied heavily on Christopher Moore's *1867: How the Fathers Made a Deal*, while Christopher Armstrong's *The Politics of Federalism: Ontario's Relations with the Federal Government, 1867–1942*, guided me through the struggles over power, literal and political, from Confederation until the Second World War. Oliver Mowat quickly emerged as the most powerful and successful defender of Ontario's interests, as A. Margaret Evans explained in her biography of Ontario's third premier. Neil McKenty aptly portrayed *Mitch Hepburn*, certainly the province's most flamboyant first minister. I also looked to Roger Graham for his life of Premier Leslie Frost; to A.K. McDougall for his book on John Robarts; and to Claire Hoy for his volume on Bill Davis. Robert Bothwell's succinct but illuminating *Short History of Ontario* was never far from my desk.

I have taken the unconventional step of citing these authors here—other valued sources are listed in the bibliography—both to acknowledge my great debt to these much-wiser minds and to avoid documentation, except for direct quotations.[2] This book, which is both a history and an argument, is intended for the general reader, one who is curious about, if sometimes confused by, the political pace of change in this former heartland, and who wants to know why Ontario's premier and the prime minister are always yelling at each other.

As well as writing books that helped to anchor mine, Sid Noel and Christopher Moore graciously agreed to review the manuscript, offering comments and criticism that greatly strengthened it. Through it all, Phyllis Bruce guided *Loyal No More* from a febrile notion to a finished manuscript. It would not have been possible without her. The text was then masterfully edited by Rosemary Shipton and ably proofread by Lorissa Sengara.

This book has also been possible because I have covered Queen's Park, the most exciting beat in Canadian politics, from the moment in 1995 when Bob Rae called the provincial election that brought Mike Harris to power until today, first for the Southam Newspapers and the *National Post*, and more recently for the *Globe and Mail*. I have been fortunate that all my editors have given me the widest latitude to explore and interpret the goings-on inside and outside the legislature, and to pursue the subject in greater depth through books.

Despite the many hands that helped in the creation of *Loyal No More*, and the many shoulders on which I stood while fashioning its argument, any outrages of fact or opinion that remain are entirely of my own doing.

Index